PAUL TILLICH
and the
CHRISTIAN MESSAGE

PAUL TILLICH

and the

CHRISTIAN MESSAGE

George H. Tavard

New York
CHARLES SCRIBNER'S SONS

NIHIL OBSTAT: WILLIAM J. WALSH, S.J.
CENSOR DEPUTATUS
IMPRIMATUR: ✠ JOHN WRIGHT
BISHOP OF PITTSBURGH
PITTSBURGH, PA.: 10 AUGUST 1961

The Nihil obstat *and* Imprimatur *are a declaration that a book or pamphlet
is considered to be free from doctrinal or moral error. It is not implied that those
who have granted the* Nihil obstat *and* Imprimatur *agree with the contents,
opinions or statements expressed.*

ACKNOWLEDGMENTS

The author is grateful to the following publishers for permission to quote from the works of Paul Tillich as indicated:

HARPER AND BROTHERS, from *Dynamics of Faith*. Copyright © 1957 Paul Tillich.

HOLT, RINEHART AND WINSTON, INC., from *The Religious Situation*, translated by H. Richard Niebuhr. Copyright 1932 Holt, Rinehart and Winston, Inc. Copyright © 1960 H. Richard Niebuhr.

THE MACMILLAN COMPANY, from *The Theology of Paul Tillich*, edited by Charles W. Kegley and Robert W. Bretell. Copyright 1952 The Macmillan Company.

OXFORD UNIVERSITY PRESS, from *Love, Power and Justice*, and *Theology of Culture*.

CHARLES SCRIBNER'S SONS, from *The Interpretation of History*, translated by N. A. Rasetzki and Elsa L. Talmey (Copyright 1936 Charles Scribner's Sons); *The Shaking of the Foundations* (Copyright 1948 Charles Scribner's Sons); *The New Being* (Copyright 1955 Paul Tillich).

THE UNIVERSITY OF CHICAGO PRESS, from *Biblical Religion and The Search for Ultimate Reality* (Copyright 1955 The University of Chicago); *The Protestant Era* (Copyright 1948 The University of Chicago); *Systematic Theology*, Volumes I and II (Copyright 1951, 1957 The University of Chicago Press).

YALE UNIVERSITY PRESS, from *The Courage To Be*.

FOREWORD

THE genesis of the present volume needs a few words of explanation. During the summer of 1953 I toyed with the idea of writing a book on the theology of Paul Tillich. Later, however, other concerns became more important. I gave up the idea of a book, although, then and later, I touched upon Tillich's doctrine in some articles.[1]

The second volume of Tillich's *Systematic Theology* was published in 1957. It expounded the Christological part of his system. Until that time I felt that Tillich's points of view could be reconciled with the faith of the Church as regards the central Christian message, the Christ himself. Reading *Systematic Theology* II made such an understanding of his doctrine impossible. Some Protestant reviewers took issue with Tillich's interpretation of Christianity. Yet no major rebuttal came. This could mean either that most theologians found Tillich's Christology unimportant or that they feared to tackle a dominant figure of the contemporary scene in American Protestantism. Which of these hypotheses fitted the facts, I do not know.

Be that as it may, the present volume tries to assess Tillich's Christology. It does so mainly in the light of Catholic theology, yet on a number of occasions I have drawn on the Christology of the Protestant Reformers, especially Calvin. This study is both expository and critical of Tillich's ideas as I understand them. It is, nevertheless, not negative. I have tried to balance what seems to be the good and the bad in Tillich's thought. The last chapter

---

[1] "The Unconditional Concern: The Theology of Paul Tillich," *Thought* (Vol. XXVIII, n. 109, Summer, 1953, pp. 234-246); "Christianity and the Philosophies of Existence," *Theological Studies* (March, 1957, pp. 1-16); "Le thème de la Cité de Dieu dans le protestantisme américain," *Revue des Etudes Augustiniennes* (1959, pp. 207-221).

endeavours to point to a way along which Tillich's valid intuitions could be used in the framework of a fully Catholic Christology.

Acknowledgements are due to the editors of *Thought*, who gave permission to incorporate into Chapter II large sections of my article of 1953, and to Mr George McGibney, who typed the manuscript.

GEORGE H. TAVARD

Mount Mercy College,
Pittsburgh, Pennsylvania.

CONTENTS

PAUL TILLICH

and the

CHRISTIAN MESSAGE

Chapter I

THE MIND OF PAUL TILLICH

IT IS hardly possible to appreciate the thought of a prominent thinker if one is unacquainted with his life. What matters most is not so much in what exterior events he has been involved, as what interpretation his conscience has given them. A purely objective judgment on a doctrine would then be misleading. For it would bypass the major driving power of that doctrine, which is to be found in the subjective intention of the thinker. What he means is a prerequisite of what he does. No doubt, what he does stands by itself once it has been made public. It belongs to the world, which is entitled to judge it according to its own standards. This alienation of any thought that one ventures to communicate to others is part of the cross that all writers and speakers, like all artists in their various fields, have to bear.

Yet it is not enough to know a doctrine in itself. The critic who wants to be fair to an author must try to obtain an insight into doctrine as a process of the mind that fathered it. The genesis of thought should reveal the intentionality of its product. This product may indeed misrepresent the underlying intention. It acquires a life of its own, which may cut many of the strings that tie it to its origin. This may be the fault of the author himself. He may have been unfortunate in the expressions that he chose. Yet it may also be the responsibility of his readers. They have not paid him enough attention; they have misread his words; they have substituted their interpretations for what he actually said; they have understood his writings in a situation that was totally foreign to his own. The only way to check the accuracy of our judgment is to trace the growing process in which his doctrine was shaped.

The following study of the Christology of Paul Tillich strives to be strictly objective. His views will be judged according to the objective standards of traditional theology, for the simple reason that I believe in the existence of objective criteria in Christological matters. The norm of Christology cannot be the new insights that theologians may reach; it must always be the consistent interpretation of Jesus the Christ that has developed in the Church along the lines set by the orthodox Fathers in the theological controversies of the early centuries of Christianity. Should Tillich's Christology stray from this standard, it must be branded as a betrayal of the Christ himself. Some readers will presumably criticize this point of view as an outmoded fundamentalism; yet it has no relationship that I am willing to recognize with fundamentalist theology. Others, without going so far, will call it a doctrinal conservatism that seems to do away with the possibility of new understandings and interpretations of the Revelation; this I would accept with some qualifications. Others still may claim that I have not fully entered into the subjectivity of my topic. To a certain extent they will be right. One person's mind remains opaque to another; or at least it is never completely transparent.

Yet I have tried not to forget the first lines of this chapter. An objective judgment should leave room for an appreciation of the subjective purpose of an author. Fortunately for the critic of Tillich's theology, Tillich himself, in several essays, has opened his mind to us. He has analysed the workings of his intellect with the utmost clarity desirable, and with an introspective power of which few men seem to be capable. He has thus provided us with a key to the structure of his thought as it has been shaped in the existential predicament of his life. In order to understand him, we will let him speak for himself as much as possible.

The first autobiographical essay to which we should refer is entitled "On the Boundary." It forms the opening chapter of *The Interpretation of History* (1936), Paul Tillich's first volume after his emigration from Germany to America in 1933. In this article Tillich looked back over an eventful past. The traumatic experience of leaving his country at the age of forty-seven sharpened his insight. It also coloured his style with what may have been regret, and what may also be a sublimation of existential reflection into delicate poetry.

A second autobiographical essay was published in 1948 as an introduction to *The Protestant Era*. It covers mainly the period of Tillich's life that followed the First World War. Though it takes the form of a reflection on the theological situation rather than on the events of his own life, the essay is relevant as an analysis of his thought between the wars.

A third essay, "Autobiographical Reflections," written for the symposium *The Theology of Paul Tillich* (1952, edited by Charles W. Kegley and Robert W. Bretall), surveys his life and experience, commenting on the philosophical and theological insights of each successive phase.

Outside of these sources, there are relevant remarks in "The Conquest of Intellectual Provincialism: Europe and America," an article included in *Theology of Culture* (1959). Tillich's comparison of America and Germany occasions reminiscences from his German years and from the time of his arrival in the United States.

Three phases may be distinguished in the development of Paul Tillich's thought.[1] The first, with which we are now concerned, roughly coincides with his life before the First World War. It has been described by him as taking place "on the boundary."[2] We may accept his judgment that he has always been living on the boundary between two temperaments, that of the Rhineland, inherited from his mother, and that of Prussia, from his father.

---

1. See Walter M. Horton, "Tillich's Role in Contemporary Theology," and Theodor Siegfried, "The Significance of the Theology of Paul Tillich for the German Situation" (in *The Theology of Paul Tillich*, 1952, edited by Charles W. Kegley and Robert W. Bretall, respectively pp. 26-47 and 68-83); Walter Leibrecht, "The Life and Mind of Paul Tillich" (in Walter Leibrecht, ed., *Religion and Culture. Essays in Honor of Paul Tillich*, 1959, pp. 3-27); Christoph Rhein, *Paul Tillich, Philosoph und Theologe: eine Einführung in sein Denken*, 1957; Max Huber, *Jesus Christus als Erlöser in der liberalen Theologie*, 1956 (Paul Tillich, pp. 223-234).

2. *The Interpretation of History*, p. 3.

We may also note that from his early childhood Tillich lived on the boundary between city and country. These remarks are not irrelevant; for a boundary situation is ideal for a mediator. "The border-line is the true propitious place for acquiring knowledge," as Tillich insists.[3] A boundary does not merely divide; it also hyphenates, uniting two positions in an existential contrast. A border-line separates two countries between which it also mediates. Thus the kind of knowledge acquired there is not haphazard.

Born in 1886, Tillich in many ways belongs to the nineteenth century. "I am one of those in my generation who, in spite of the radicalism with which they have criticized the nineteenth century, often feel a longing for its stability, its liberalism, its unbroken cultural tradition."[4] Yet he has also been deeply marked by the doom of the twentieth century, with its fantastic contrasts, its upheavals, its dilemmas. "It has been my fate, in almost every direction, to stand between alternative possibilities of existence, to be completely at home in neither, to take no definitive stand against either."[5] A "German by nature," deeply attached to his country "in the sense of landscape, language, tradition and common experience of historical fate,"[6] he was destined in later life to pitch his tent in an alien land and to make it his home, never forgetting the European culture he represents and mediates in this new environment. Thus Tillich's thinking developed first as a mediation-philosophy. He describes it as standing on a multifold boundary, hence as attempting a multifold mediation, "between social classes, between reality and imagination, between theory and practice, between heteronomy and autonomy, between theology and philosophy, between Church and society, between religion and culture, between Lutheranism and socialism, between idealism and Marxism."[7]

It is not by accident that Tillich began his career as a philosopher rather than as a theologian. As a philosopher of culture and of religion, he lived his vocation of standing on a border-line. Philosophy, especially when it is primarily concerned with

3. *Ibid.*   4. *The Theology of Paul Tillich*, p. 3.
5. *The Interpretation of History*, p. 3.   6. *Ibid.*, p. 69.
7. These are the headings of the main sections of the essay "On the Boundary."

culture and religion, is naturally mediative, much more so than theology. Later, when Tillich turned more specifically to theology —a shift made unavoidable by the development of his philosophy of religion—it was understandable that he should first have been drawn to the so-called "mediating theology" of Protestant liberalism. In philosophy, Schelling, whom he studied for a Ph.D., and in theology his professor Martin Kaehler, shaped his thought more profoundly than anyone else. From them he learnt that "dialectics" is the most efficient way of promoting "the task of theology," which "is mediation."[8] Dialectics is not to be confused with the so-called "dialectical theology" of Karl Barth. The dialectical thought of Tillich antedates the work of Barth and has a totally different meaning: "Dialectics is the way of seeking for truth by talking with others from different points of view, through 'yes' and 'no,' until a 'yes' has been reached which is hardened in the fire of many 'no's' and which unites the elements of truth promoted in the discussion."[9] Tillich listened to the voices that were able to say 'yes' and 'no' at the same time, in order to mediate in the direction of 'no' without surrendering their 'yes' and vice versa. "Mediation does not mean surrender."[10] Nor does it mean building walls where bridges are needed. Thus Tillich felt uncomfortable with "the Ritschlian theology, which establishes an infinite gap between nature and personality." On the contrary, he confides, "This is the reason for the tremendous impact that Schelling's philosophy of nature has made upon me —although I was well aware that this philosophy was scientifically impossible."[11]

This desire to reconcile philosophy, religion and science and to affirm their insights together in total loyalty to each extended itself to the field of arts. On the "boundary between reality and imagination," Tillich penetrated this world through literature and, later, through painting. "The discovery of painting was for me an experience of decisive importance."[12] Moreover, the search for integration of all the fields of human intuition contributed to Tillich's appreciation of Roman Catholicism. "My

8. *The Protestant Era*, p. xiii. 9. *Ibid.* 10. *Ibid.*, p. xiv.
11. *The Theology of Paul Tillich*, p. 4. 12. *The Interpretation of History*, p. 15.

growing inclination toward the old Church and her solutions of the problems of 'God and the world,' 'state and Church,' were nourished by the overwhelming impression made upon me by early Christian art in Italy. What no amount of study of Church history had brought about was accomplished by the mosaics in ancient Roman basilicas."[13] Tillich has continued to be attracted to the older forms of Catholicism, in its early centuries as well as in the Middle Ages, which represented to him the only far-reaching attempt to steer the course of mankind beyond autonomy and heteronomy, towards what he calls "theonomy." At one time in his life he even considered it a meaningful possibility to join the Catholic Church. It seemed for a moment, in the early period of Nazism, that the choice lay between two unequal evils: "Only once in my life the thought of possibly joining Catholicism penetrated into a deeper realm of my consciousness—even if not the deepest—when, during the year 1933, prior to the resurgence of German Protestantism, the alternative seemed to confront me, between either Christian or heathen Catholicism, the Roman Church or national heathenism in Protestant garb."[14] Catholicism in modern times has lost its theonomous structure. It now is "the most potent system of religious heteronomy."[15] Yet at times the theonomy from which Roman Catholicism derives attempts to break through. Then we can envisage again, looking into the past, what a Catholic theonomy could be in the future. Thus Paul Tillich wrote in 1928: "The Catholic Church has manifestly been able to preserve a genuine substance that continues to exist, although it is encased in an ever hardening crust. But whenever the hardness and crust are broken through and the substance becomes visible, it exercises a peculiar fascination; then we see what was once the life-substance and inheritance of us all and what we have lost, and a deep yearning awakens in us for the departed youth of our culture."[16]

Far from bringing him into the Catholic synthesis, Tillich's search led him to a reinterpretation of Protestantism. Early in his studies, under the influence of his masters at the University

13. *Ibid.*, p. 16.   14. *Ibid.*, p. 25.
15. *Ibid.*, p. 24.   16. *The Protestant Era*, p. 194.

of Halle and especially of Martin Kaehler and Wilhelm Lütgert, he discovered the universal validity of Protestantism. The synthesis he was looking for was given in the Protestant principle, if only Protestants could become aware of it. The tension he experienced on the boundary line of his life was overcome in what may best be described as a religious ecstasy. "The result of this tension was either a decision against the one or the other side, or a general scepticism or a split-consciousness which drove one to attempt to overcome the conflict constructively. The latter way, the way of synthesis, was my own way."[17] Tillich perceived that in the Protestant Reformation lay an insight that could open all doors and resolve all conflicts. Accordingly, he did not work as a pure philosopher, but as a philosopher-theologian. Only twice had he taught theology before his arrival in the United States. Except for five years as *privatdozent* in theology at the University of Berlin (1919-1924) and one year at Marburg (1924-1925), his academic home had always been in philosophy, at Dresden, Leipzig or Frankfurt. "Nevertheless," he states, "I was and I am a theologian, because the existential question of our ultimate concern and the existential answer of the Christian message are and always have been predominant in my spiritual life."[18]

We now reach the second phase of Paul Tillich's intellectual development. The synthesis which he had hoped to build between culture and religion in the framework of the German philosophical and Christian tradition was shattered by the First World War. Paul Tillich's experiences as an Army chaplain on the Western Front destroyed the illusion of an easy mediation between the antinomies of life and culture. The individual thinker as the man who could build such a synthesis was no longer a possible figure. The world of individualism was sinking. "The First World War was the end of my period of preparation. Together with my whole generation, I was grasped by the overwhelming experience of a nation-wide community—of the end of a merely individualistic and predominantly theoretical existence."[19] The

17. *The Theology of Paul Tillich*, p. 10.   18. *Ibid.*   19. *Ibid.*, p. 12.

early collective enthusiasm of a nation at war opened possibilities for a collective existence hitherto unsuspected, an insight which remained even after the hardships of a four-year long war of positions had revealed grimmer aspects of reality. "After a few months I became convinced that the war would last indefinitely and ruin all Europe."[19a] Yet the idea of a collective existence persisted, to be achieved on another, profounder, level than that of national unity.

Paul Tillich became professor of philosophy shortly after returning from the Front upon the defeat of his country and during the chaos of an abortive revolution. His religious quest for a synthesis continued. He still believed in the possible realization on earth of the Protestant principle. He was not so naïve as to think that socialism, in any of its forms, could approximate the Kingdom of God: "The realization of the Kingdom of Justice and Peace within this existence is impossible. The Kingdom of God can never become an immanent reality and the absolute can never be realized in space and time."[20] Yet in a period of socialist reconstruction, theology should hold up the ideal of the Kingdom of God before the eyes of the builders. Tillich had always experienced "the boundary between social classes." Though born into the bourgeoisie, he had been in contact with both "the old nobility"[21] and the lower classes, an experience that "prevented me from becoming myself bourgeois." Awareness of the social problem and the shattering of the illusion of an easy mediation between the many tensions of existence led him to attempt a synthesis between the old theonomous wisdom of the Middle Ages and the new socialistic concepts: "I made the attempt to incorporate into socialism those elements of the feudal tradition which have an inward affinity with the socialist idea."[22] Already as a philosopher Tillich stood "on the boundary between idealism and Marxism"; he now found himself at another boundary, "between Lutheranism and socialism." While he could not share the utopian dreams of socialism, he approved its immediate purpose of reshaping society. Socialism stressed the importance of

19a. *Ibid.*
21. *Ibid.*, p. 9.

20. *The Interpretation of History*, p. 56.
22. *Ibid.*

history, and precisely in history Tillich discovered the dominant motif of his philosophical and theological thought. "History became the central problem of my theology and philosophy because of the historical reality as I found it when I returned from the First World War: a chaotic Germany and Europe; the end of the period of the victorious bourgeoisie and of the nineteenth-century way of life; the split between the Lutheran Churches and the proletariat; the gap between the transcendent message of traditional Christianity and the immanent hopes of the revolutionary movements."[23]

The meaning of a historical period, what Tillich called its *kairos*,[24] may be revealed by the events taking place in it. Tillich believed that the socialist movement unveiled the meaning, the inner intentionality, of the post-war years. In this interpretation of the times, which he labelled "religious socialism," the "movement towards something, towards the new, which is claimed as well as expected, is constitutive" of history.[25] Thus socialism entered into a symbiosis with Tillich's previous concern for a theonomy based on the Protestant principle. Socialism was thought to be the starting-point of a drive towards a new theonomy. It was the latest avatar of the Protestant principle. "Socialism is to be understood as one such beginning towards a new theonomy. It is more than a new economic system. It is a total system of existence. It is the form of theonomy demanded and expected in the present *kairos*."[26] Tillich did not identify himself with the Socialist Party, which was little concerned with any aspect of religion. "In my heart I have never belonged, and do not belong to any party, because the most important point in the political realm seems to me to be one which is never expressed in political parties, except in distorted forms. My longing has been and is a 'fellowship' which is bound to no party, although it stands nearer to the one than the other, and which shall be the vanguard for a more righteous social order in the spirit of prophecy and in accord with the demand of the *kairos*."[27]

23. *The Protestant Era*, p. xvii.
24. See Chapter V.
25. *The Interpretation of History*, p. 59.
26. *Ibid.*, pp. 59–60.
27. *Ibid.*, p. 67.

In the post-war period Paul Tillich developed many of his earlier insights. The notions of the Protestant principle, of ultimate concern, of the *kairos*, of the demonic, took final shape in his mind. He began working on his *Systematic Theology* at Marburg in 1925,[28] and naturally acquainted himself with the new philosophical and theological trends. He accepted the spread of psychoanalysis from the outset, and saw in its analyses a confirmation of his notion of the demonic and of the salvific power of the Protestant principle.

Of his relationship with existential philosophy Tillich speaks in several different ways. In "On the Boundary," he stresses with what readiness he accepted this new way of thinking during his professorship at Marburg, where also Martin Heidegger was teaching. "I myself was prepared in a threefold way to accept this philosophy": Tillich was familiar with the last period of Schelling; he was acquainted with Kierkegaard; and he had been influenced by "the philosophy of life."[29] And again: "It was easy for me . . . to accept the analysis of human existence as given by Kierkegaard and Heidegger."[30]

In "Autobiographical Reflections," however, Tillich mentions resisting Existentialism when he was exposed to it at Marburg: "It took years before I became fully aware of the impact of this encounter on my own thinking. I resisted, I tried to learn, I accepted the new way of thinking more than the answers it gave."[31]

Between these two accounts (1936 and 1952) Tillich gave a third version of his connection with Existentialism. He not only "accepted" the existential analysis of man; he himself formulated an existential interpretation of history, as seen in his article on "Existential Philosophy" (1944). There his religious socialism of the post-war period is presented as a form of existential philosophy: "The third and contemporary form of existential philosophy has resulted from a combination of this philosophy of life' with Husserl's shift of emphasis from existent objects to the mind that makes them its objects, and with the rediscovery of Kierke-

28. *The Theology of Paul Tillich*, p. 14.   29. *The Interpretation of History*, p. 39.
30. *Ibid.*, p. 32.   31. *The Theology of Paul Tillich*, p. 14.

gaard and of the early developments of Marx. On the one hand Heidegger and Jaspers, on the other the existential interpretation of history found in German 'religious socialism' are the main representatives of this third period of the philosophy of experienced Existence."[32]

The other main current of that time was the growth of the so-called "dialectical" or "neo-orthodox" theology of the Swiss theologian Karl Barth. Tillich never fully belonged to this major theological effort. Yet for a time he could be considered one of the rather loose group of "dialectical" theologians who thought along the lines of Barth's *Commentary on the Epistle to the Romans* in its first edition (1919). The Karl Barth of 1919 was still strongly marked by Protestant liberalism. He searched for an organic relationship between God and creation. Precisely this point lies at the core of Tillich's conception of a theology of culture. If this was the "dialectic" of Karl Barth, Tillich was a dialectical theologian. He remained with Barth until the Barthian dialectic began to give way to neo-orthodoxy. The second edition of Barth's *Commentary on the Epistle to the Romans* (1922) blew up the bridges which the first edition had erected between God and nature. The organic link of Creator and creature had become an abyss. Beyond this point Tillich could no longer follow Barth, which he made clear in several articles in 1923 and 1924.[33] His strictures on neo-orthodoxy became sharper with time, reaching a climax in his article, "What Is Wrong with the 'Dialectic' Theology?" (1935).[34] The gist of this criticism is paradoxically expressed in the following warning: "The Grand Inquisitor is about to enter the Confessing Church, and strictly speaking with a

---

32. *Theology of Culture*, p. 79. Though Tillich's thought is clearly existential, it cannot be identified with Existentialism itself: Tillich is not a disciple of Heidegger or Sartre, Jaspers or Camus.
33. See "Kritisches und positives Paradox. Eine Auseinandersetzung mit Karl Barth und Friedrich Gogarten" (in *Theologische Blatter*, II, n. 11, Nov. 1923, pp. 263-69); "Antwort" (*Ibid.*, n. 12, Dec. 1923, pp. 296-99). Karl Barth's answer to Tillich's first article is also *Ibid.*, n. 12, pp. 287-96: "Von der Paradoxie des positiven Paradoxes. Antwort und Fragen an Paul Tillich."
34. *Journal of Religion*, April, 1935, pp. 127-45.

strong but tight-fitting armour of Barthian supranaturalism."[35]
This post-war period was the most productive in Tillich's life.
No doubt he published more books after his arrival in the United
States and especially after the Second World War, yet all his ideas
had come to fruition during his teaching years in Germany,
where he articulated them in numerous lectures, often made into
articles. He also published three books of importance. *Das System
der Wissenschaften* (1923) embodied some of his insights concerning
the philosophy of culture and of religion. What may be his master-
piece, *Die religiöse Lage der Gegenwart* (1925),[36] was a splendid
survey of the modern cultural situation, plumbing its religious
depths. Finally, just before the Nazis seized power, appeared a
small volume on socialism, *Die sozialistische Entscheidung* (1933).
Its publication proved the undoing of Tillich's career in Germany.
Thus his efforts on behalf of a religious transformation of socialism
in the direction of a future theonomy came to an end with the
advent of Adolf Hitler. In that fatal year, 1933, Paul Tillich
arrived in New York City.

A third period in Tillich's life and activity now opened in
the new political and religious situation of America. Politically,
Tillich was progressively led to abandon his active fight for,
though not his concern with, religious socialism, a movement
which had found no hearing in America. Intellectually, his interest
in *kairos* and in the sense of the present historical moment receded
into the background of his thinking. Theologically, Tillich passed
from the level of the philosophy of religion to that of theology
proper: his new responsibility as lecturer in systematic theology
at Union Seminary in New York City involved him more and
more in directly theological problems and discussions. The focus
of this development was the formulation of his *Systematic Theology*.

Tillich has clearly set forth his experience of emigrating.
Living on "the boundary between home and alien land" long
before he had to change his home, he had made it part of his
creed that a Christian "is to leave his own country over and over

35. *The Interpretation of History*, p. 26.
36. English translation: *The Religious Situation*, 1932, reprinted in 1956.

again, and to go into a land that is shown unto him, and to trust the promise which is for him purely transcendent."[37] This conviction drew him beyond the narrow confines of nationalism. His being-a-German had always meant being-a-man. "Mankind as such is a symbol for that which lies beyond history, the Kingdom of God, in which the border between home and alien land has ceased to be a border."[38]

The endeavour then to root himself in the American soil entailed many shifts in Tillich's concerns. He became aware of American Protestant thought. Looking back in 1953 upon this discovery, Tillich wrote that German Protestantism was more provincial than its American counterpart[39] but that American Protestant culture understresses theology: "Theology is not dismissed, but it is reduced to a secondary role."[40] And American theology itself concentrates on social ethics rather than on history or dogma. The multiplicity of American Churches has given American Protestantism "world-wide horizons" and a more "catholic" dimension than would otherwise be possible. Now this happens to correspond to "one of the main problems" of Tillich's theology, "namely Protestant principle and Catholic substance."[41] In other words, Tillich found a number of congenial trends in American Protestant culture. "The America to which we came was wide open."[42] It was so wide open that he found in it a larger audience than Germany had granted him.

Yet a certain restriction of Tillich's activities became necessary. Circumstances forced him to narrow the range of his acquaintances. "For external and practical reasons, it became impossible to maintain the relationship to artists, poets and writers which I enjoyed in post-war Germany."[40] Artists, poets and writers in America had less contacts than in Europe with the formal academic life of universities. Instead, Tillich's interest in psychoanalysis grew as a result of the impact of this discipline on American life. "I have been in permanent contact with the depth-psychology movement and with many of its representatives,

37. *The Interpretation of History*, p. 68.   38. *Ibid.*, p. 72.
39. *Theology of Culture*, pp. 160 ff.   40. *Ibid.*, p. 165.
41. *Ibid.*, p. 169.   42. *Ibid.*, p. 176.   43. *The Theology of Paul Tillich*, p. 18.

especially in the last ten years.[44] The problem of the relation between the theological and the psychotherapeutic understanding of men has come more and more into the forefront of my interest."[45] With the spread of "demythologization" in the years following World War II, Tillich had occasion to renew, on a theological level, his concern for arts, symbols and myths. Thus what had been denied him in terms of personal contacts with artists was restored to him in terms of theological discussions.

The following chapters will be devoted to an analysis of the central message of Paul Tillich's American writings. There is therefore no need to list them at this point. I merely note the appearance of the first two volumes of his *Systematic Theology*. The work begun at Marburg in 1925 thus reached completion in New York in 1951 and 1957.

Tillich's life and times, as portrayed in this short survey, show us his intellect as that of a "philosopher of life" whose field of research has been the relationship of religion to existence. The manifold aspects of religion and of existence have corresponded to the numerous "border situations" into which destiny has thrown Tillich since 1886. Thus he has learnt, through reflection and especially through the experience of both success and disappointment, that all religion and all existence stand or fall with their ultimate commitment. Facing the Unconditional, all life is lived on a border-line. In unity with the Unconditional, all boundary situations are ultimate. "To stand on many border-lines means to experience in many forms the unrest, insecurity and inner limitation of existence, and to know the inability of attaining serenity, security and perfection. That is true of life as well as of thought. . . . But . . . there is a boundary of human activity which is no longer the dividing line between two possibilities, but a limitation through that which is beyond any human possibility—the Good and the True. In its presence, even the very centre of our being is only a boundary, and our utmost perfection only a fragment."[46]

44. i.e., since 1942.   45. *The Theology of Paul Tillich*, p. 18.
46. *The Interpretation of History*, p. 73.

Chapter II

THE UNCONDITIONAL CONCERN

THE function of theology, Catholic or Protestant, is to purify the faith of believers through an enlightened criticism of empirical Christianity. Catholic theology achieves this—or should achieve it were theologians always conscious of their function—through a self-criticism whereby the theologian brings his own Christianity as thought and experience in line with the requirements of the Word of God spoken in Scripture and echoed in the Church of yesterday and today. Thence, from man to man, from teacher to student, from lecturer to listener, from writer to reader, a continuous self-reformation tends to spread abroad. This is why all great theology is prophetic. Announcing the Word of God, it prepares the members of the Church to receive it in its pureness, as the Baptist prepared his disciples for the coming of Christ. While never speaking in the name of the Church, a prophetic theology gives the lead to the Church of tomorrow by helping men to welcome the hierarchal teaching into a fully scriptural and traditional background.

Paul Tillich has tried to build a prophetic theology for the twentieth century on a Protestant basis. In order to understand many of his positions, a study of his conception of theology as expounded at the beginning of *Systematic Theology* is required. It is perfectly true that "method and system determine each other" and that "no method can be developed without a prior knowledge of the object to which it is applied."[1] This would make a definitive appreciation of his theological method impossible before one is acquainted with his whole system. Yet another viewpoint would

1. *Systematic Theology* I, p. 60.

15

hold that an insight into the formal structure of his theology ought to reveal, however incompletely and schematically, the whole scope of his systematic elaboration. Only within such a general framework do Tillich's concept of faith and his Christology make sense.

The search for a theological norm underlies all attempts to give a theological interpretation of Christianity. Whether one tries to write a *summa*, an essay or a system—according to a distinction mentioned by Tillich[2]—one consciously or unconsciously desires to hold on to a thread that will give theology a texture in keeping with the requirements of faith and of intelligibility. In theological thought a norm is the standard to which everything will be compared, the measure by which all will be measured. Accordingly, it ought to possess certain qualifications, the most obvious being, besides truth—this we may take for granted here—self-evidence. For the norm will judge all that comes in contact with it. The theologian must have it always at hand and be ever ready to let others judge his contentions by means of it. The self-evidence in question is obviously not identical with rational clarity; it rather belongs to the spontaneous implications of the Christian faith.

The history of theology shows several norms being used successively by theologians or schools.

Throughout the patristic era the groundwork for theological thinking was provided by the sense of mystery which grasps anybody approaching the being of God. The Fathers upheld the transcendence of God in the framework of their knowledge of him, not only by what they wrote or said, but also by their attitude while speaking of him. "Neither the prophets of whom I speak," St Gregory Nazianzen wrote, "nor any of the others stood in the substance or essence of God, as the Scriptures testify; they did not see or explain the nature of God."[3] The norm of theology is then the cloud that enshrouds God's glory. Guided by the Spirit the believer seeks "theo-logy," knowledge of God, intimacy with him, inside faith and its darkness. Theological contemplation is a symposium of knowledge and no-knowledge.

Speaking generally, the medieval theologians shifted the norm

2. *Ibid.*, p. vii.   3. Gregory Nazianzen, *Oratio* 28, 19; P.G., 36, 52.

of theology from the level of an anagogical awareness of the presence of God in his absence to the level of a sacramental experience of creation. Everything is then reduced to the sacramentalism of creation, of which the Christian sacraments form the acme. All things, whether natural or supernatural, are images of God, mirrors wherefrom the face of the Christ beckons to men to take up their cross and follow him. Temporality is a prism through which eternity is seen.

In Catholic theology there is a close relationship between the theological norm thus understood and the object or subject matter of theology. Scholastic nomenclature called subject matter the viewpoint prevailing in a given theology and from which things are considered. Thus Aquinas wanted to judge everything from the standpoint of "God," Bonaventure from the standpoint of "the credible in its promotion to intelligibility." Yet both evolved their theologies within the framework of the sacramentalism of creation. Their so-called subject matter derived from diverse emphases in their perception of the sacramental norm, referring to God as God (St Thomas) or to God as Light of the intellect (St Bonaventure).

The function of a norm in Protestant theology would be wider than in Catholic theology. Whereas the latter would acknowledge a "rule of faith" which transcends theology even when it is assumed in it, the former would be free to recognize a similar rule or to erect its theological norm into a norm of belief. The distinction between the realm of faith and the realm of theology, which is so sharp in Catholicism, would then be blurred, if not altogether erased. To a certain extent a Protestant theological norm may be equated with Revelation: it is Revelation as seen in a certain era and area.

With these preliminary remarks in mind, we may share Tillich's eagerness to find a theological norm which is adequate for today. Where can we discover such a norm? It must be not only objectively sound, that is, immediately focused upon the centre of the Christian message, but also subjectively efficient, suited to modern men's requirements and needs. It must be recognizable by all who share in the Christian experience and it

must furthermore appeal to those who do not consciously partake
of it.

Tillich's starting-point in his quest for a theological norm is
both Paulinian and Lutheran. "Justification by faith" is asserted
by St Paul as being the summary of his Gospel and is taken up by
Luther as the norm of his thinking. A Protestant tradition may be
called Lutheran precisely insofar as it makes justification by faith
—whatever this may mean—the kernel of its *kerygma*, the heart
of its preaching. Coming from the Lutheran tradition, Tillich
derives the main intuition of his theology from Luther's view of
justification. But his acquaintance with the topsy-turviness of the
modern situation makes him look for an application of the
Protestant principle to the realm of the intellect. By vindicating
justification by faith alone, as opposed to a supposedly Catholic
doctrine of justification by works, Luther condensed on a
particularly sensitive point the Protestant principle that every
man-made action, formulation or idea must be protested against
inasmuch as it tends to undermine God's transcendence (and it
necessarily does so). This universal protest entails an affirmation
of the universal power of God. It must protest even against
itself, whenever justification by faith is shifted from the status of a
principle to that of a doctrinal datum. Tillich's understanding
of this principle places him on the road to a theological norm valid
for modern times. For he holds that the principle of protest, of
justification by faith, not only justifies man's experience as sinner
and just at the same time (*simul peccator et justus*); it also justifies
his experience as right and mistaken at the same time, as having
the truth and denying it, as believing and doubting. Justification
by faith opens the realm of the intellect to the dominion of Christ
alone. When we are farthest from God we are nearest to him.
When we profess atheism we believe. For our adhesion to
intellectual truth is not man-made; it is the outcome of our
justification by grace alone. The principle of protest must make
us deny man's self-complacency in respect to beliefs or doctrines
that he can grasp and label his own. It must urge us to affirm God's
victory in man's defeat, God's truth in man's untruth. No

intellectual work justifies; what justifies the intellect is faith alone, grace alone.

A theological norm may now be proposed. It will not be any man-formulated doctrine, like sacramentalism. It will not even be justification by faith as a doctrinal panacea (for this also would call for protest). It will be something which is beyond all protest because it is the ground from which all protest stems and the power that makes protest valid. When he justifies by grace, the Incarnate Word makes man into a new being, which has substance in him alone and is perceived by faith alone. This *New Being* is the norm of theology. But let us be careful lest the Protestant protest indict us even here. The *New Being* comes from Jesus. Yet it flows from his universal function as the Christ, as showing forth the divine, as mediating the infinite. It is related to Jesus as the Christ, that is, as interpreted by faith alone. Among medieval theologians the question was often raised: Is theology concerned with Christ? or as we would say, Is it "Christocentric"? Tillich would have no difficulty in saying that it is indeed Christocentric, but he would protest with all the prophetic power of the Protestant principle against a "Jesucentric" theology. The theology that deals with the historical Revelation is not concerned with the pronouncements of Jesus—we do not know them, anyway, since the New Testament is already the witness of faith —but with the role of Jesus as the Christ, as bearer of the *New Being* for every man and every creature, beyond what man has formulated concerning that *New Being*, beyond even man's consciousness of it.

If the *New Being* in Jesus as the Christ is adopted as theological norm, there follow some important consequences for theology. We will come later to the problem of the sources wherefrom theology draws its material. For the time being I wish to point out that such a theology is essentially Christian, since it is in Jesus as Christ that man is justified by grace and assumed into a *New Being*. "He who is Christ is he who brings the new eon, the new reality."[4] Yet it is not merely biblical, for the Bible itself is

4. *Systematic Theology* I, p. 49.

norm must be apprehended as an answer to man's situation, as *the* name for the ultimate ground of being. This is why Tillichian theology follows a "method of correlation" wherein an "existential analysis," a "transcendent realism," lays bare man's ultimate concern and proceeds to show that the *New Being* in Jesus as the Christ is the God-given answer to man's questions, the unfolding of his situation, the justification by grace of his existence.

When man is ultimately concerned, when he has reached the bottom of being and has given himself to it, even though in doubt and with hesitancy—for these belong to his situation as man— then he is indeed justified by faith. Whether he knows it or not, whether he has heard of Christ or not, he is then grasped by the *New Being*. For this is the Protestant protest: to assert God in the midst of the demonic, the Unconditional amidst the conditioned. This is justification by grace alone: to be taken hold of by the Christ *now*, not doctrinally but existentially, not in theory but in fact. Every unconditional concern stamps a man as having been reached by the *New Being in Christ*, by "a reality in which the self-estrangement of our existence is overcome, a reality of reconciliation and reunion, of creativity, meaning and hope."[9] Adhesion to the Unconditional resolves the contradictions of the conditions of existence. Then the *New Being* re-establishes the "courage to be," which is "rooted in the God who appears when God has disappeared in the anxiety of doubt."[10] Then man is justified by grace alone.

If we want to pinpoint the whole of Tillichian theology, we can hardly find a better view of it than this: it consists in bringing to light the unconditional concern of man and in showing the identity of the Unconditional, with which man is concerned, with the *New Being* manifested in Jesus as the Christ. Hence the norm of Tillich's theology is best expressed thus: "The material norm of systematic theology today" is "the *New Being* in Jesus as the Christ as our ultimate concern."[11] Theology is interested in this ultimate or unconditional concern in itself. In the Christian faith it is equated with Christ himself as the revealer of the *New Being*.

9. *Systematic Theology* I, p. 49.   10. *The Courage to Be*, p. 190.
11. *Systematic Theology* I, p. 50.

Others formulate it differently. A Buddhist, for instance, would connect it with the essence of Buddha; a Marxist, with the historical process. These symbols could be dismissed as lacking objective validity, yet it is relevant that both the Buddhist and the Marxist exhibit an unconditional concern. Theology today has to show them Christ as the Revelation of the Unconditional.

The Christian quality of Tillichian theology is therefore most radical. But this Christianity is to be identified neither with any Christian Church nor with Christendom as a whole. It embraces both Jesus as the Christ and what Clement called the "Logos spermatikos." Every theology knows that there is a sense and a manner in which God is not limited by the Church, that Christ reaches men outside of those who are official members of the Church. Tillich's theology drives this principle to an ultimate logical implication: whether they are aware of it or not, Christ is the unconditional concern of all men. Theology has to point him out as that unconditional concern. It has to do it even when it is impossible to call him by his name. Every ultimate concern, every protest in the name of the Unconditional against any kind of idolatry—of things, of nations, of doctrines—implies a share in the Christian witness.

This explains the messianic eloquence which now and again comes to the surface in the writings of Paul Tillich. Many pages of *The Protestant Era* betray a deep-rooted conviction of the Christian victory in man's defeat, in the Church's defeat, in Christendom's defeat. This is no opinion. It is the faith itself in the *New Being* in Christ which seeks expression in the most meaningless situations as it brings justification in the heart marked by sin, in the mind smeared by unbelief.

Tillich's theological norm entails an attitude concerning the sources of theological thinking.

All documents that present an avenue of approach to the unconditional concern of man are to be used as sources of theology. First those which speak of Christ as the Revelation of the Unconditional among men. Granted that "the task of systematic theology is to explain the contents of the Christian faith,"[12] those contents

12. *Ibid.*, p. 34.

—the datum, as Catholic theologians would say—have to be focused upon the norm adopted by theology and streamlined according to that norm. Hence the twin principles upon which Tillich selects his sources. On the one hand all documents are used, the Bible first, but also the events and records of Church history—Orthodox and Catholic texts included—and even "the material presented by the history of religion and culture."[13] On the other hand, none of them may be erected into a norm. All are to be judged by the theological norm. No statement in any source is "infallible." No council or pope or biblical excerpt is, as such, a standard. Yet all are sources insofar as they speak of the *New Being* in Jesus as the Christ. "The biblical message would not have become a message for anyone, including the theologian himself, without the experiencing participation of the Church and of every Christian."[14] In this sense Tillich's theology admits that "tradition" is valuable, though by no means normative in its own right. Like the Bible itself, it may be the occasion for perceiving the theological norm, whenever the power of the *New Being* is sensed in it. This follows logically from the nature of the theological norm. Catholic theology would consider traditional elements as normative only insofar as they share in the power of the *New Being*. But no Catholic theologian would rely on himself alone to discern that power; he would trust the collectivity of the faithful and appeal to the totality of Christian experience.

The streamlining that has just been mentioned, the judgment of the sources by reference to the theological norm, has to be effected and pronounced by the theologian himself. It implies that he has experience of both, that he partakes not only of a knowledge of the Bible, of Church history and of the history of religion and culture, but also of the *New Being*. He must be unconditionally concerned.

This raises a question that seems to be the crux of Tillichian theology. "Experience is the medium through which the sources 'speak' to us, through which we can receive them."[15] It is not a

13. *Ibid.*, p. 38.   14. *Ibid.*, p. 35.
15. *Ibid.*, p. 40.

source, for it can bring nothing new; yet it has a productive power. In this position I fail to see a perfect consistency. Tillich holds that "experience receives and does not produce. Its productive power is restricted to the transformation of what is given to it. But this transformation is not intended. The act of reception intends to receive and only to receive. If transformation is intended, the reception becomes a falsification."[16] Nevertheless he adds, "The influence of the medium, the experience of the theologian, should not be so small that the result is a repetition instead of a transformation, and it should not be so large that the result is a new production instead of a transformation."[17] If this means that there is always a transformation when the Christian message is received, even in spite of the receiver's intentions, there is no difficulty. If it means that such an unintentional transformation is needed by the message or for a more adequate presentation of it, I am not sure how it can avoid being a new production. Presumably, Tillich's answer would refer me to the theological norm: a mere transformation—unintentional—would respect the source's relation to the *New Being* in the Christ whereas a new production would warp it. As he explains elsewhere, revelation as such is ended; the revelatory process still goes on.[18] Catholics would call it "development."

Yet this is not all, for the *New Being* itself is mediated through the theologian's experience. "The norm grows within the medium of experience. . . . It is at the same time the criterion of any experience. The norm judges the medium in which it grows; it judges the weak, interrupted, distorted character of all religious experience, although it is only through this feeble medium that a norm can come into existence at all."[19] As Tillich says, "collective as well as individual experiences are the mediums through which the message is received, coloured and interpreted."[20] Reception and colouration refer us to the sources; interpretation to their judgment by the norm. But this judgment is existential, mediated by the theologian's experience. In what measure does this mediat-

16. *Ibid.*, p. 46.   17. *Ibid.*
18. *Ibid.*, p. 144.   19. *Ibid.*, p. 52.
20. *Ibid.*

ing experience "transform" it? In itself the *New Being* in the Christ is never grasped by any theologian; it rather grasps him. Yet the theologian judges in the name of the *New Being*. Luther pronounced that the Epistle of St James was insufficiently relevant to the *New Being*. How did he know?

Theology involves risk. The greatest danger that threatens theologians is to make their *personal experience* of the *New Being* in Christ the theological norm. Then theology is self-condemned, for it is no longer the *New Being* as such which judges the sources of theology and which is shown as the unconditional concern of man. Personal experience is always conditioned; its substitution for the Unconditional would be a form of idolatry. And history shows that the Protestant protest has not always been at work against this fairly common tendency of Protestant theology. Tillich knows this. Yet we might wish that he had elaborated further on the mediation of the theological norm by the theologian's experience. Ultimately his theology will stand or fall on this point. Justification by faith ensures God's victory in man's error, but it would bulwark no theologian against an eventual misinterpretation of the *New Being* in Jesus as the Christ.

Our central problem will precisely be to discover if Paul Tillich's understanding of the mystery of Christ is faithful to the Christology of the Catholic tradition. It is true that Tillich borrows many of his cues from traditional formulations of doctrine, as in his Trinitarian analysis of the *New Being*. The *New Being* in Jesus as the Christ places us in the power of the Living God. Our being is rooted in the abysmal ground of being which classical theology calls the Father. It is created through the meaningful and form-giving Logos. It is unified in the "dynamic unity of depth and form"[21] which is the Spirit. Because "the doctrine of revelation is based on a Trinitarian interpretation of the divine life and its self-manifestation,"[22] the theology of the unconditional concern is developed according to the threefold existential scheme of being, existence, and life. At each stage a creaturely reality existentially experienced calls for, and is answered by, ultimate Being, ultimate Existence, and ultimate Life. Classical nomen-

21. *Ibid.*, p. 156.   22. *Ibid.*, p. 157.

clature calls these Father, Word, and Spirit. When Paul Tillich unfolds his systematic theology, he intends us to discover the Trinitarian life.

Yet this is not the final answer to the question that I have posed concerning the experiential medium of his theological norm. If a theologian interprets his experience of the *New Being* as a participation in the life of God, in the ultimate Life, the intentionality of his theology is valid. But his intention may not be fulfilled throughout his theological system. In particular, there comes a point where theology has to be either Catholic or Protestant. A Catholic would never trust his own thinking on the ground that he has been grasped by the life of God: how could *my* consciousness of this be a valid objective norm? He trusts his thinking because he is at one with the collective Christian experience as witnessed to in the life of the Church as a whole. The Catholic theological norm transcends its mediation by the theologian in a communion with the Whole. The *New Being* in Jesus as the Christ must be interpreted in the totality of Christian experience, not that of one man only but that of all Christians of all times. Since Christianity is qualitative rather than quantitative, nothing less than a structural Whole can express it. In this sense, theology has to choose between the Church as the realm of Catholicity (or *New Being*) and the Church as an empirical, temporary and fallible witness to the gospel of the *New Being* in the Christ.

At this point, the principles of Tillich's theological reflection profess not to be Catholic. As a result, they run the risk of being dependent on one man's experience of the *New Being* in the Christ rather than on the experience of the whole of redeemed mankind.

Paul Tillich develops his Christology around his central notion of unconditional concern. In classical Christology, belief in Christ and the acceptance of salvation are described as "acts of faith." The Christ is the objective reality or Person that we reach in the subjective experience of faith. In order to grasp Tillich's Christology, we must therefore assess his conception of faith as a Christian experience.

Chapter III

FAITH AS PROTEST AND ACCEPTANCE

TILLICH'S formulation of the Protestant principle widens the perspective of the Reformers. For Luther as for Calvin, justification by faith was meaningful only in the context of Christian existence. Given the life of faith in the community of the Church, the reception of the sacraments rightly administered and the audition of the Word of God soundly preached, a Christian was defined as one who is saved by grace through his faith in Jesus Christ, the Saviour. The Saviour speaks to him in the Word and comes to him in the sacraments.

Tillich does not deny this. On the contrary, we shall see that for him Christianity more than any other faith or community is the realm of the Protestant principle. Nevertheless he is not content with asserting salvation by faith, unless salvation truly reaches to the depths of man. To an extent that was unknown or even unsuspected by the Reformers, the modern world has sounded these depths. The drama of subconscious conflicts, the split in the consciousness of existence reflected in the existentialist philosophies, the ideological wars of our century, the anguish surfacing in modern art and literature: these are tokens of a dramatic humanism which leaves the Reformers far behind. If it is universally valid, the Protestant principle of justification by faith must be extended to these largely uncharted areas. Tillich believes that he has achieved its full extension by applying it not only to the doctrinal, social, and moral conditions of salvation, but also to the unconscious domain of man's reception of the message of redemption. The first Protestant gesture affirmed God's graciousness beyond and above human merit: this was the task of the sixteenth century. The second affirms God's graciousness in spite of man's intellectual doubts. The third affirms God's graciousness even within man's existential split. These last two steps are the task of our century.

The centre of Tillich's intuition may also be expressed in this way: man's unconditional concern is the subjective response to the Protestant call to protest. An analysis of religion, of literature, of philosophy, of culture, of love, would reveal that men experience an unconditional concern. Whatever they believe or disbelieve, they touch a realm in their self-awareness which escapes doubt or belief. If justification is an act of God, man's unconditional concern is the acceptance by man of his justification even in the midst of questionings and doubts. For questions belong to the intellect, but this concern lies beyond the intellect, in what Tillich calls "the depths of reason." We are saved neither by merit nor by belief, but by the Unconditional. This term, in Tillich's words, "points to that element in every religious experience which makes it religious. . . . It characterizes that which is our ultimate and consequently unconditional concern, whether we call it 'God' or 'Being as such' or 'the Good as such' or 'the True as such,' or whether we give it any other name. . . . Unconditional is a quality which we experience in encountering reality, for instance, in the unconditional character of the voice of conscience, the logical as well as the moral."[1]

This description of the Unconditional as a quality, and not a being, brings us to an important fact: "Nobody can have the ultimate, nothing conditioned can possess the Unconditional."[2] This undercuts every attempt to identify the Unconditional directly. The Unconditional is not "a God"; it is not a being. It is, rather, some quality of the self of which we have an indirect experience. Were it only a quality of the self, it would be ours, yours and mine, but as we, you and I, are conditioned and, as such, unable to possess the Unconditional, the fact that we experience total commitment, ultimate devotion, unconditional concern, points to a complementary aspect of existence: that the Unconditional is both in us and beyond us. Grace is not a possession; it is only received through faith. Likewise, man's unconditional concerns, in as far as they are truly unconditional, reach both

1. *The Protestant Era*, p. 32, n. 1.   2. *Ibid.*, p. 171.

the rock bottom of self and a transcendental element which dominates the self. Two worlds touch at this point. Jesus "praises the poor in so far as they live in *two* worlds, the present world and the world to come. And he threatens the rich in so far as they live in one world alone."[3] This makes for the unchanging greatness of the Psalms. For what the Psalmist expresses is that "the Presence of the centre of all life within the centre of *his* life implies both a radical attack on his existence, and the ultimate meaning of his existence. We are known in a depth of darkness through which we ourselves do not even dare to look. And at the same time, we are seen in a height of a fullness which surpasses our highest vision."[4] Nothing matters; yet everything is supremely important "if it has an unconditioned meaning, an unconditioned depth, an unconditioned reality."[5]

Unconditional concern implies this "infinite tension"[6] between the conditions of our existence and the commitment to an unconditional element; it entails "daring and risk."[7] This, in Tillich's theology, is faith: "Faith is the state of being ultimately concerned."[8] The principle of justification by faith alone, as Tillich explains it, contains more than strikes the eye. As understood by Luther, it meant faith in Christ as the Saviour. The *Greater Catechism* reads: "I believe that Jesus Christ, the true Son of God, has been made my Lord, . . . that through his blood he has liberated me from my sins, from the Devil, from death and from all misfortune."[9] With Tillich we are on a different level: not *what* is believed matters, but *how*. To say that faith is an assent to an extrinsic revelation is to distort it. But this intellectual distortion would be a form of idolatry, just as the emotional distortion which makes faith an outlet for our subjective feelings. Faith is something else. It cannot be pinned down to one set of beliefs or identified with one emotional experience. These distortions of faith are corrected by the Protestant principle that nothing conditioned may vehicle the Unconditional. Rather,

3. *The Shaking of the Foundations*, p. 27.   4. *Ibid.*, p. 50.
5. *The Religious Situation*, p. 35.   6. *The Shaking of the Foundations*, p. 50.
7. *The Protestant Era*, p. 215.   8. *Dynamics of Faith*, p. 1.
9. *Cat. Maj.*, P. II, a. 2, n. 27.

faith underlies every belief and every emotion: it is the total commitment of man to ultimacy, "the total surrender of him who accepts this claim [of ultimacy],"[10] the "concern about our existence in its ultimate 'whence' and 'whither.' "[11]

Should one ask, "*what* is the Ultimate?," an answer may be sought in the fact that men have devised a multitude of faiths; they have identified the Ultimate with this God or that; they have worshipped symbols of the ultimate. Though perhaps mutually exclusive, all these tend to the same point: total commitment. Tillich frequently divides these "religions" into four groups: paganism, Judaism, Christianity, humanism. Each in turn contains a multitude of sub-groupings. Clearly, however, this is not an answer to the question. But can there be one? Can a man, under the conditions of existence, identify the Unconditional? All these forms of religion are "tools"; yet the Unconditional cannot be a tool. Is then religion at all possible?

Paul Tillich's analysis of faith provides his answer to this basic question. Every faith may be seen from two angles. As existential commitment, unconditional or ultimate concern, all faiths coincide; they are faith. Insofar as they try to identify the Unconditional, they differ. The two standpoints should be carefully distinguished. For a faith which interprets the Unconditional, even if it distorts its own interior dynamics, is valid insofar as it is a total commitment. With this total commitment we are now concerned.

To speak of commitment makes no sense if we do not complete the statement by answering the question: commitment to what? Tillich speaks often of "total commitment," "unconditional concern," "infinite passion" without telling us what one is committed to, what the concern is about, and what the passion aims at. This infuriates some of his readers. And little wonder: systematic shunning of the objective question (commitment to what?) leaves a bewildering after-taste of word-juggling. Once the great words Unconditioned, Ultimate, Absolute, and the like, have been

10. *Dynamics of Faith*, p. 1.
11. *Biblical Religion and the Search for Ultimate Reality*, p. 15.

spoken, there are those who sit back and admire. But Tillich would be the last to be pleased by being made into an "authority." He does not use words without a meaning; he does not avoid a question without pointing, at least implicitly, to the fact that the question contains its own answer, if only we are able to read it correctly. Not that Tillich always refuses to answer. A large section of his *Dynamics of Faith* deals with this. "The term 'ultimate concern' unites the subjective and the objective side of the act of faith—the *fides qua creditur* (the Faith through which one believes) and the *fides quae creditur* (the faith which is believed)."[11a] While he uses these classical terms, Tillich also transcends the level at which the question is raised. Along with the total theological tradition, he recognizes that "the one side cannot be without the other. There is no faith without a content toward which it is directed."[12] But classical theology, whether Catholic or Protestant, would next proceed to identify this object, or content, of faith in terms of God, or Christ, or the Church, or Revelation, according to different points of view. In any case, the content of faith would be distinct from the human act of assent or acceptance. Even when theology insists that faith is "infused," as a free gift from God, it distinguishes the content, or object, of faith from that infusion. In the words of St Paul, "faith comes by hearing."[13] In scholasticism, faith comes from God's intervention, though its object is perceived through the Church's ministration. In classical Protestantism, faith likewise remains distinct from its object, salvation by Christ.

Tillich strikes out on a new path. The distinction between subject and object in faith disappears in his theology. The dichotomy between the believer and the Revelation shrinks. "In terms like ultimate, unconditional, infinite, absolute, the difference between subjectivity and objectivity is overcome. The ultimate of the act of faith, and the ultimate that is meant in the act of faith are one and the same." There takes place a "disappearance of the ordinary subject-object scheme in the experience of the Ultimate, the Unconditional. In the act of faith that which is the source of this act is present beyond the cleavage of subject

11a. *Dynamics of Faith*, p. 10.   12. *Ibid.*   13. Rom. 10. 17.

and object. It is present as both and beyond both."[14] This at least is clear: Tillich believes that the act of faith is both subject and object. We have faith that we have faith: if this is believed unconditionally, if we are to surrender totally to this experience of having faith in faith, of believing belief, then we truly have faith. If our surrender is not total, then our faith is false, our commitment hypocritical.

This borders on the absurd. But we should remember that language is always inadequate to express the Unconditioned. Faith is unconditional surrender, and as such it can only be expressed paradoxically, or symbolically. The paradox is that faith is its own object. The symbol says that we believe in God, meaning that what we believe is a newly discovered dimension of self, a trans-self, the eternal ground of self. Here subject and object are no longer distinct.

If this is faith, there must be an element in man which faith has unveiled; hence this impression of assenting to something new, of Revelation. Because it looks new, it assumes the function of an object towards which we reach. It conveys a mysterious sense of the holy. In this context faith is "ecstatic," hungering after "the ecstatic attraction and fascination of everything in which ultimacy is manifested."[15] Because they had this experience the prophets of the Old Testament described God as "the creative ground of everything and in everything, who is always present, always creating and destroying, always experienced as nearer to ourselves than we ourselves are, always unapproachable, holy, fascinating, terrifying, the ground and meaning of everything that is. This is the living God, dynamic in himself, life as the ground of life. . . ."[16] Yet, let us not be mistaken. An experience of the holy is not an experience of otherness. The holy is not outside of us. Faith does not tie us to some extrinsic deity above and beyond us. The holy was there before we discovered it. It belongs to the structure of our existence.

The existential experience through which faith breaks into

14. *Dynamics of Faith*, p. 11.   15. *Ibid.*, p. 113.
16. "Jewish Influences on Contemporary Christian Theology" (*Cross Currents*, New York, Spring 1952, pp. 35-42), quotation p. 40.

human life is "estrangement." "There is no faith without an intrinsic 'in spite of' and the courageous affirmation of oneself in the state of ultimate concern. . . . Existential doubt and faith are poles of the same reality, the state of ultimate concern."[17] Faith is the positive realization of what is negatively expressed in terms of estrangement. Whoever plunges into himself breaks through the surface and sinks from depth to depth. The wise men of all ages "have found that they were not what they believed themselves to be."[18] The drama of man is that he is not what he believes himself to be. There is a disruption between essence and existence which Tillich analyses at length. There are all sorts of disruptions in our psychical depths which he also analyses. In *Systematic Theology* II, estrangement is described as "unbelief," as *hybris*, as concupiscence, as a "separation of freedom from destiny," of "dynamics from force," of "individualization from participation." The "vanity of human existence"[19] has been universally described and deplored. Life does not appear as a unity, but as a conundrum. The "puzzling fragments of life" have to be deciphered.[20] And this is all the more difficult as "every man is a fragment himself . . . a riddle to himself."[21] Existential philosophers have analysed estrangement and anguish more thoroughly than had been done before, and have reached nearer to the meaning of faith than many others. Tillich's descriptions of Existentialism are reminiscent of his description of faith. "The existential thinker is the interested or passionate thinker. . . . The passionately living man knows the true nature of man and life."[22] "Interest, passion, indirect communication": these are the qualities of the existential thinker.[23] Are they not also those of the faithful?

They are and yet they are not. The existential philosopher who describes the negative depths of life does only part of what faith achieves. Philosophy as such can probe depths. But only faith can pierce through them and reach the point where depth is

17. *Dynamics of Faith*, pp. 21-22.   18. *The Shaking of the Foundations*, p. 56.
19. *The New Being*, p. 168.   20. *The Shaking of the Foundations*, p. 111.
21. *Ibid.*   22. *Theology of Culture*, pp. 89-90.
23. *Ibid.*, p. 91.

also height. It is proper to faith to realize that there is no estrangement without an underlying unity. "The absolutely strange
cannot enter into a communion. But the estranged is striving for
reunion. . . . Estrangement presupposes original oneness."[24] This
is true of reunion among men and especially of human love. It
is also true of faith. Faith sees estrangement as the manifestation
in our existence of our original unity. Its ultimate commitment
is a commitment to that from which we are estranged and to
which we remain nevertheless related. Speaking in terms of God,
we shall say that "infinite passion for God is, no less than the
sexual passion, a consequence of the objective situation, namely,
of the state of separation of those who belong together and are
driven towards each other in love."[25] This then is the experience
of faith: to experience that estrangement in all its forms as a veil
covering our union with God, the ground of our being. Seen
from inside the experience of faith, estrangement represents both
original union and future reunion.

Tillich can be eloquent when dramatizing man's existential
estrangement.

> The state of our whole life is estrangement from others and
> ourselves, because we are estranged from the Ground of our
> being, because we are estranged from the origin and aim of our
> life. And we do not know where we have come from, or
> where we are going. We are separated from the mystery, the
> depth and the greatness of our existence. We hear the voice
> of that depth; but our ears are closed. We feel that something
> radical, total and unconditioned is demanded of us; but we
> rebel against it, try to escape its urgency, and will not accept
> its promise. . . . Sin in its most profound sense, sin as despair,
> abounds amongst us.[26]

Yet in spite of "meaninglessness, emptiness, doubt and cynic-
ism" it is possible to say "in spite." "Sometimes it happens that
we receive the power to say 'yes' to ourselves, that peace enters
into us and makes us whole, that self-hate and self-content
disappear, and that our self is reunited with itself. Then we can

24. *Love, Power and Justice*, p. 25.   25. *Ibid.*, p. 27.
26. *The Shaking of the Foundations*, p. 160.

say that grace has come upon us."[27] This is the experience of faith: to accept estrangement to the point where it becomes union.

> It is as though a voice were saying: "You are accepted. *You are accepted*, accepted by that which is greater than you, and the name of which you do not know. Do not ask for the name now; perhaps you will find it later. Do not try to do anything now; perhaps later you will do much. Do not seek anything. *Simply accept the fact that you are accepted*." If that happens to us we experience grace.[28]

Faith thus appears to be the acceptance of being accepted, and it is analysed as such in *The Courage to Be*. In other words, it is the acceptance of estrangement, the acceptance of sin. Sin and grace, or sin and faith, belong together like estrangement and union. Faith is the awareness that they are one. Then estrangement is reunion; despair is hope; anxiety is peace. Man has "the certainty of total forgiveness in the situation of total guilt."[29]

This reversal of values is beautifully illustrated in the sermon, "Is There Any Word from the Lord?"[30] Faith is the word from the Lord which breaks through the human situation and transforms it. It does not "add something to our situation," yet it adds "a dimension to the dimension in which we ordinarily live."[31] Faith is from above, since it is from the Lord, or at least it seems so to the mythical imagination. In reality "the word from the Lord is the word which speaks out of the depth of our situation. It is, one could say, the deepest meaning of the situation."[32] This faith changes nothing in the circumstances and the structure of life. Yet it reverses our attitude. "The word from the Lord, the voice out of the depth of our situation, ends the anxiety of the possible and gives the courage to affirm the real with its many questionable elements."[33] At this stage right and wrong may be interchanged: "If you realize that in relation to God man is always wrong, your wrong may turn out to be right."[34] Faith

27. *Ibid.*, p. 163.
28. *Ibid.*, p. 162.
29. *Systematic Theology* II, p. 58.
30. *The New Being*, pp. 114-124.
31. *Ibid.*, p. 118.
32. *Ibid.*
33. *Ibid.*, p. 119.
34. *Ibid.*

is the ecstatic discovery that despair is meaningful; it is the experiential knowledge that wrong is also right; it is the certainty that doubt too is belief.

Before going further in this analysis of Tillich's concept of faith, I should voice a basic criticism. The plumbing of existential depth which Tillich places at the core of faith is not a distinctly Christian phenomenon. All philosophers have tried to reach the bottom of man's self-awareness. They have attempted to overcome the distinction between essence and existence, to resorb the difference between subject and object. That all this has been done since philosophy began is not surprising: for this effort is none other than that of making ourselves like God. Unity with God is a natural desire which is at least implicit in the heart of man. Men may or may not be able to give a name to God. At any rate, they tend to God as the goal of their fulfilment. They seek him in the dark along the winding roads of their anxieties, through the ups and downs of their fevers. And there is a sense in which the words that Pascal places on the lips of the Lord are true: "You would not seek for me, had you not already found me." Tillich's description of faith, when it describes man's seeking and inclining towards God, is extremely valuable.

Yet, as we have seen, man's search for God remains essentially ambiguous. The coincidence of guilt and forgiveness may be understood in two ways: either guilt is subsumed in forgiveness, or guilt already is forgiveness. An option between these two interpretations completely changes the meaning of guilt. Or, take faith as the acceptance of being accepted. If we are accepted, we are accepted, whether we accept it or not. What does our acceptance add to our being accepted? Strictly nothing. The conscious element of faith (our acceptance) is tacked on to a more basic element (our being accepted). If Tillich thinks he is being radical in seeing this acceptance as faith, his radicalism can be outdone: faith is our being accepted. Everything is accepted; all is love; all is forgiveness. It is better, for our own peace, to know this experientially; but at bottom it makes no difference. We are accepted in any case. Faith is no longer a free act of man's entire personality. It is the stuff of all human life. Tillich comes dangerously near to saying this when he underlines the universality of faith: "Every religious and cultural group and, to a certain extent, every individual is the bearer of a special experience and content of faith." [35] "There is no human being without an ultimate concern and, in this sense, without faith."[36] If every man cannot help having faith, what is unique in the Christian faith? Between classical theology, Catholic or Protestant, and Tillich something has intervened. What has happened is that Tillich has ontologized the concept of faith. Catholicism, followed by the Reformation, sees faith as a freely accepted act. Man can reject faith. It is also an act of God: God enlightens the soul; and the soul, accepting or rejecting this light, believes or disbelieves. With Tillich, faith underlies everything. Doubt itself stems from underlying faith. Only faith can attempt to refute faith. "Our ultimate concern can destroy us as it can heal us. . . . But we never can be without it."[37] Some men are distinguished from others, not in that they freely accept God's light and believe, but rather in that they suddenly, ecstatically, realize what is common to all, though hidden, namely, that estrangement is also reunion, that life has an ultimate meaning.

Now we are reaching the crux of Tillich's theology of faith. The faith of both the New and the Old Testament is selective, subtracting men from the kingdom of this world and adding them to that of heaven. It leaves man *in* the world but takes care to make him not *of* the world where he lives as a stranger and pilgrim inhabiting no permanent city. It unites him to the holy community of the Church, and in doing so breaks his ties with the unholy community of the world. In this Church there is neither Jew nor Gentile, neither male nor female, but only if one has abandoned a world where Jews and Gentiles are foes, and male and female try to dominate each other. Faith implies separation: a man from his brother, a daughter from her mother.

The faith of Paul Tillich is the exact opposite. Instead of erecting the holy community out of the world, it sees the whole world as already being the holy community. Nobody escapes it.

35. *Dynamics of Faith*, p. 55.   36. *Ibid.*, p. 114.   37. *Ibid.*, p. 16.

All, even unawares, belong to it. Is this still the Christian faith?

Tillich begins with the traditional distinction between subjective and objective faith. In classical theology, the former results from a divine light which is freely accepted. It formally constitutes the saving element of faith. But this subjective faith cannot be analysed alone, for it never exists without an object. This object, as we have said, comes from the Church: we are told what the Church believes and, enlightened by God, we believe it too. In scholastic terms, subjective and objective faith are likened to form and matter; and as philosophers know, there is neither form without matter, nor matter without form. The Reformation, with its dislike of scholasticism, avoided these terms; but it maintained their purpose: subjective faith was essentially correlative to objective belief.

Where a distinction existed, Tillich sees a separation. He studies subjective faith as though it leads an independent existence. Admittedly, he maintains that faith always has a concrete content. "The content matters infinitely for the life of the believer, but it does not matter for the formal definition of faith."[38] We thus face a strange paradox: what matters infinitely for the believer does not concern the nature of his faith. How can this be, if faith is infinite concern? Tillich has analysed subjective faith as though it could stand by itself, without a concrete content. There is nothing in faith but faith itself: what he calls "absolute faith" is "the accepting of the acceptance without somebody or something that accepts."[39] Even when he defines faith by its relation to the Unconditional, he does not give it an object. Thus, speaking of "the unconditional demand upon those who are aware of something unconditional," he has to correct this statement by a dialectical recourse to negation: "Neither 'the Unconditioned' nor 'something unconditional' is meant as a being, not even the highest being, not even God."[40] Yet faith cannot exist without a man believing something, without a subject and an object. Tillich has therefore been led to discover a content in it: an ultimate concern about life. From all his analyses he has concluded that faith is the true reading of man's existential estrange-

38. *Ibid.*, p. 4.   39. *The Courage to Be*, p. 185.   40. *Theology of Culture*, p. 24.

ment as a relating estrangement, as a healing wound. This means that he has given faith a preliminary content distinct from its concrete content. Thus faith appears on three levels: as subjective it is ultimate concern; as content of this concern, it is reunion in estrangement, forgiveness in guilt, ground of being in separation from this ground; as objective, related to a concrete content, it is still a third phenomenon.

We must go further in our criticism. So far we have discovered a methodological distortion that has resulted in a description of faith whose Christian character may be called questionable. By way of corroboration let us now investigate a connected point. It will show that Tillich's analysis of faith has obliged him to distort a basic element of Christian belief: original sin.

Tillich's treatise on the "fall of man" is contained in the second volume of his *Systematic Theology* as part of his description of existence and of the existential conditions that inspire man's desire for salvation or, in Tillich's words, his "quest for the Christ." The Christian doctrine of original sin, as understood by Tillich, is a theological explanation of estrangement. As such it belongs to Christology: Christ, by hypothesis, will bring salvation from this basic anguish of existence. It belongs *a fortiori* to a theology of faith. If faith implies awareness of estrangement and courage to endorse and bear estrangement, it also implies knowledge of "original sin" and rests on the experience of the fall of man. What the myth of the Fall tells of mankind in general, faith discovers in each man: that existence is tragic, and that this tragic element, if accepted, becomes a way to holiness and peace. In such a perspective, faith experiences the Fall.

Tillich's treatment of the Fall is superior to many others in trying to meet the philosophers half way. It duly recognizes that philosophical intuition opens insights into sin. It happily borrows from psychology its description of a state before the Fall as "dreaming innocence,"[41] distinguished from awakeness and from experience. But the "dreaming innocence" of Tillich is not anterior to a subsequent event which would give the acquired knowledge of good and evil. It is the psychological background

41. *Systematic Theology* II, p. 33.

of all human acts. Human actions mark a passage from the "dreaming innocence" of one who has not been subjected to the conditions of human existence to the wide-awake experience of man in existence. In other words, the state before the Fall corresponds, in mythological language, to what philosophers call essence. The choice between good and evil corresponds to existence itself. This "leap from essence to existence"[42] is a universal fact, but is not a fact distinct from creation. Every human being, by the very fact that he is created, is in existence. As such he is in a state of wide-awake experience; he has the experiential knowledge of good and evil as soon as he is able to act humanly. Original sin is not original in the sense that the first man sinned and that from this we derive the fact that we are born sinners. "The notion of a moment *in* time in which man and nature were changed from good to evil is absurd, and it has no foundation in experience or revelation."[43] Tillich is aware of the danger of this identification of sin and creation; his critics have voiced the "justified fear that sin may become a rational necessity."[44] It is all the more puzzling that, having adequately formulated this objection, he does not answer it.

The Fall of man is, for Tillich, the transition from uncreated essence, or non-being, to created existence, or being. This happens to every man. Every man is caught in the following tragedy: no exercise of his faculties is possible without the experience of estrangement from his essence in God, that is, without sin.

Now, the trouble with this is that it certainly is not the meaning of Revelation. That a theologian should argue against the Fall as a primordial catastrophe of the human race on the basis that "it has no foundation in experience" is disconcerting, for no supporter of this classical Christian belief has ever claimed that we have experience of it. It would be as absurd to base the Fall of the First Man on present-day experience as it would be childish to deny that Fall arguing from the absence of a direct experience of it by mankind today. This is an amazing flaw in Tillich's theological method. To make matters worse, Tillich finds that an original Fall "has no foundation in revelation."

42. *Ibid.*, p. 44.   43. *Ibid.*   44. *Ibid.*

It is significant that Tillich's account is exclusively based on Genesis and on the story of Adam and Eve's eating of the forbidden fruit in the Garden of Eden. Yet it is recognized by exegetes that if Genesis tells a story of the first sin, it does not speak of the transmission of that sin. The Old Testament had no notion of original sin as taught by Christianity. It had a notion of the sin of Adam and that his descendants, imitating their forefathers, have also sinned, but it never suspected that there could be a causal link between Adam's sin and man's being born in sin. On the contrary, rabbinical tradition taught, and still teaches, that man is born without sin. It is not on Genesis, but on St Paul, that the Christian view is founded. Calvin spoke for the entire Christian tradition when he grounded the doctrine of the Fall of Man on Romans 5.18: "As the fault of one has brought condemnation on all men, so the righteousness of one brings on all a lifegiving righteousness." St Paul knows the Fall in the light of the Redemption. They are two correlative events. The historicity of Redemption stands facing the historicity of the Fall. He who would deny the latter would by implication negate the former. Calvin rightly commented: "These words are not obscure: that several are justified through the obedience of Christ, as they have been constituted sinners through the disobedience of Adam; and accordingly, that just as Adam, enfolding us in his ruin, has caused our perdition, likewise Christ brings us back to salvation through his grace. I do not think that a longer proof is needed in such a clear light of truth."[45]

By overlooking the Pauline doctrine, Tillich can treat the entire doctrine of the Fall as mythical. This helps him to ontologize original sin. It has been done at the cost of a clearly scriptural teaching, and by rejecting a whole stream of tradition, from the time of the Fathers through the period of the Reformers down to our own time—all for the purpose of bringing the notion of original sin in line with Tillich's analysis of estrangement. In classical Christianity, faith implies the assumption of man into redemption by Christ, his purification from the stain of original sin contracted in the First Man. In Tillichian Christianity, faith

45. *Institutes*, Book II, ch. 1, n. 6.

remains saving; it saves from estrangement by revealing that estrangement is, after all, not estranging. This estrangement is "sin," incurred by the very fact that we are created. The correlation of faith and sin remains; the classical language may be used, but voided of its substance.

There is no faith, for Tillich, without a concrete content, corresponding to the objective knowledge of Revelation in classical theology, but with him the traditional terms have been "given a radical reinterpretation."[46] Briefly stated, the formulas in which faith conveys its concrete content are only symbolic attempts to identify the Unconditioned. Granting, as Tillich has painstakingly explained and as he repeats time and time again, that the real purpose of faith is to grasp "the power of being, conquering non-being," to experience "our ultimate concern," this purpose "expresses itself in symbols and myths which point to the depth of reason and its mystery."[47] Objective statements of faith, whether made inside or outside the Christian tradition, are symbols and myths, pointers to the ultimate ground of being, to the absolute meaning of reality. Religion, whether pagan or Christian, is a system of symbolic statements and symbolic rites trying to express an experience of the Unconditioned.

Tillich's vocabulary varies. Sometimes he will identify religion and faith as the ultimate vital ecstasy: "Religion is the state of being grasped by the power of being-itself." As such it is a universal phenomenon lying at the root of atheism, agnosticism and the loftiest mysticism: faith tends to become the stuff of all life. The case is the same, in this context, with religion: "In some cases the religious root is carefully covered, in others it is passionately denied; in some it is deeply hidden and in others superficially. But it is never completely absent. For everything that is participates in being-itself, and everybody has some awareness of this participation, especially in the moments in which he experiences the threat of non-being."[48] In an early book Tillich analysed the *religious situation* of his age through its implicit surfacing in

46. *Systematic Theology* I, p. 111.   47. *Ibid.*, p. 110.
48. *The Courage to Be*, p. 156.

science, metaphysics, art, politics, ethics, unchurched mysticism, and eschatological movements, before explaining the same religious situation in a survey of the Churches. The religious situation is there identified with "an unconscious, self-evident faith which lies at a deeper level than the apparent antithesis of belief and unbelief."[49]

For the most part, however, "religion" is not equated with the ultimate dynamic of faith, but rather with man's systematic ambition to give a name to the Unconditioned. This ambition is not only justified; it is also necessary to faith itself. For faith cannot be communicated unless it is couched in language; and language, if it is to be understood, must have a recognizable frame of reference. A system of speech that will express the Unconditioned by pointing to it cannot be purely intellectualistic. Tillich denounces with vigour conceptions of faith in which an "element of truth is embedded in a whole of error."[50] The root of such distortions is simply explained: "Faith as being ultimately concerned is a centred act of the whole personality. If one of the functions which constitute the totality of the personality is partly or completely identified with faith, the meaning of faith is distorted."[51] An intellectualistic bias makes faith into an act of intellectual, unconditional belief in a set of supposedly revealed, or at least infallible, statements; this distortion forgets that faith is not knowledge, but beyond knowledge. A voluntaristic over-emphasis makes faith into a product of the will-to-believe; but "no command to believe and no will to believe can create faith. . . . Finite man cannot produce the certainty which belongs to faith."[52] Finally, there are emotionalistic distortions where "faith is a matter of merely subjective emotions, without a content to be known and a demand to be obeyed."[53]

A safe course avoiding these pitfalls must be charted. The concrete content of faith, the linguistic expression of the Un-conditioned, is neither mere knowledge, nor mere will to believe or mere feeling. Connected with all three, it lies deeper than any.

49. *The Religious Situation*, p. 40.
51. *Ibid.*, p. 30.
53. *Ibid.*, p. 39.

50. *Dynamics of Faith*, p. 31.
52. *Ibid.*, p. 38.

Yet only the rational faculties can provide a distinct knowledge of anything. One must then conclude that, although it is intellectual, the process of tacking a name on the Unconditioned cannot aim at a distinct knowledge. All it can do is to devise adequate symbols and myths.

What symbols and myths represent in Tillich's universe must be related to his elaborate conception of Revelation. No concrete content of faith is man-made in the ordinary sense of the terms. One cannot invent symbols of the infinite; none can "be produced intentionally."[54] No poet can purposely set himself the task of elaborating a new symbolic of the Absolute. Rather, symbols are provided along with man's perception of the Unconditional. Those elements of the concrete universe that were present to his consciousness, or even to his unconscious, within the situation where he identified himself with an unconditional concern, may all become for him adequate symbols of his faith. In order to be meaningful to a collectivity, these symbols must be "at least accepted by the collective unconscious of the group in which they appear."[55] The peculiar experience in which the ground of being (the Unconditional) is reached and potential symbols of it are provided constitutes what Paul Tillich calls "revelation." The congeries of elements that contribute to this experience form a "revelatory situation,"[56] a "revelatory event,"[57] a "constellation of revelatory character."[58] A "revelatory event," since it is an event, can be studied historically. It is dated and located. Yet there is no new revelation with each new revelatory event: "always and everywhere there is only the one revelation,"[59] namely the manifestation of the depths of being. What strikes man as a new revelation actually is a "new awakening."[60]

Thus understood, "revelation is the manifestation of what concerns us ultimately."[61] Negatively, it opens our eyes to the "abysmal element in the ground of being";[62] it lays bare the fact that, though we are, we might not have been; this "threat of non-

54. Ibid., p. 43.   55. Ibid.   56. Systematic Theology I, p. 125.
57. Ibid., p. 127.   58. Ibid., p. 118.
59. The Interpretation of History, p. 239.
60. Ibid.   61. Systematic Theology I, p. 110.
62. Ibid.

being,"[63] or "shock of non-being,"[64] is "a necessary element in revelation."[65] Apart from it one cannot reach ultimacy, for ultimacy faces us precisely when every conditioned element of being has been discarded. What remains is then, seen from "the dark night," non-being, abyss. But a revelation that would end there would foster despair, not faith. Faith is sparked when revelation shows the positive side of the mystery of being: "as ground and not only as abyss."[66] The correlation of abyss and ground in revelation nevertheless shows how near despair may be to faith. This is beautifully expressed in the following: "The hell of despair is the strange work that love does within us in order to open us up for its own work, justification of him who is unjust."[67]

A revelatory situation always has two sides, both of which escape the ordinary superficial structure of life. We are now touching the rock bottom of being-itself. We are at the parting of nothingness and being. What then takes place is no longer simply an event; it is a "miracle"! And what is experienced is no mere experience; it is "ecstasy." Ecstasy is "the state of mind in which reason is beyond itself, that is, beyond its subject-object structure."[68] The mind then "is thrown out of its normal balance, shaken in its structure. Reason reaches its boundary line, is thrown upon itself, and then is driven again to its extreme situation."[69] What is then known is known as the Unconditional; it escapes all the conditions of common human knowledge and experience, since it underlies all of them and gives them the power to be. If inspiration "is the name for the cognitive quality of the ecstatic experience, [it] cannot mediate knowledge of finite objects or relations. It does not add anything to the complex of knowledge which is determined by the subject-object structure of reason. Inspiration opens a new dimension of knowledge, the dimension of understanding in relation to our ultimate concern and to the mystery of being."[70]

63. *Ibid.*   64. *Ibid.*
65. *Ibid.*   66. *Ibid.*
67. *Love, Power and Justice*, p. 114.
68. *Ibid.*, p. 112.   69. *Ibid.*, p. 113.
70. *Ibid.*, p. 115.

As to "miracle," it is the "sign-event"[71] which has occasioned or provoked the ecstatic awareness of revelation. It does not require special "supranatural interference in natural process."[71] The structure of natural causality is not broken. What happens is that certain natural events, when encountered in a special turn of mind, point to the mystery of being and non-being, and induce the beholder to commit himself unconditionally to this revelation. "The sign-events in which the mystery of being gives itself consist in special constellations of elements of reality in correlation with special constellations of elements of the mind."[72] Miracle occasions ecstasy; yet the event in question has become a miracle only through ecstasy. The subjective and the objective condition one another. Taking these revelatory elements together, "one can say that ecstasy is the miracle of the mind and that miracle is the ecstasy of reality."[73]

By definition, religion originates in a correlation of miracle and ecstasy. The basic problem of all religions, however, is that literally anything may be a medium of revelation. Any event may be a miracle. Tillich thinks that nature, history, groups, individuals and "the word" may be, and have been, mediums of revelation.[74] The multiplicity of revelatory situations is at the origin of many different symbols of ultimate concern which have been developed by religions. Faith is unique. But its symbols are manifold. Could there be only one symbol, there would be only one concrete content of faith, and therefore one religion. This naturally raises the problem of a "final revelation": is there one revelatory event that transcends and underlies all others? The problem of Christianity and of its universal claim is thus posited. In Tillich's problematic, no discussion of Christianity is meaningful if we leave out of sight his conception of a revelatory experience: a final revelation, if there is one, is first of all a "constellation of revelatory character."

Several passages analyse the concrete contents of faith as formulated in diverse religions, classifying them according to contrasting tendencies: historical and non-historical;[75] ontological

71. *Ibid.*, p. 116.　　72. *Ibid.*, p. 117.　　73. *Ibid.*
74. *Ibid.*, pp. 118-126.　　75. *Systematic Theology* II, p. 87.

and moral;[76] ontological and cosmological;[77] sacramental and ethical.[78] Many other points of view could be found. There is stress on negativity and void (Buddhism), on positivity and fulfilment (Brahmanism), on cosmic expression of the power of being (polytheism), on the sexual manifestation of the vital urge (Tantrism), on the demonic aspects of being (witch-cults), on the ethical implications of being (Confucius), and so on indefinitely. You could say, "What a mess!"; but you could also say, "What a wealth of symbols, all expressing man's ultimate concern, all pointing to the ground and abyss of all! What a luxuriance of revelatory situations and experiences! What devotion to man's quest for being-itself, for the New Being beyond the distinction of subject and object!"

Yet this multitude of symbols, myths, rites, creeds, scriptures and traditions raises a serious question: Is there, or should there be, a criterion to judge all these expressions of faith? Tillich's answer is: "The Unconditional, of which we are immediately aware if we turn our minds to it. The criterion of every concrete expression of our ultimate concern is the degree to which the concreteness of the concern is in unity with its ultimacy."[79] The prophet whose preaching creates for his disciples a new symbol of the Unconditional, and the priest who ritually uses accepted symbols of faith and worship both run a great risk. "It is the danger of every embodiment of the unconditional element, religious and secular, that it elevates something conditioned, a symbol, an institution, a movement as such to ultimacy."[80] Yet it is the greatness of religion that "it tries to surpass the given reality in order to approach the unconditional."[81] Should there be a *final* revelation, or a universal set of religious symbols, it would be such a revelation, and such a symbol, as would negate itself most completely at the very moment when it reveals the Unconditional most positively. A perfect symbol of the Unconditioned "is no longer self-subsistent as it seemed to be before; it has become transparent

76. *Dynamics of Faith*, pp. 58-69.   77. *Theology of Culture*, pp. 12-27.
78. "Jewish Influences on Contemporary Christian Theology," p. 40.
79. *Theology of Culture*, p. 29.   80. *Ibid.*
81. *The Protestant Era*, p. 79.

or, as we could say, 'theonomous.' "[82] A religion focused on such a symbol would be a "self-transcending realism";[83] it "experiences the ultimate in and through a concrete historical situation and denies any degrees of approximation to it, knowing that it is always, at the same time, unconditionally near and unconditionally far."[84] The theology of faith thus reaches a point where intelligent discussion must focus on the symbol of the Cross as a self-denying positiveness, that is, on the revelatory meaning of "Jesus as the Christ."

Paul Tillich has certainly made a remarkable effort to define faith in terms that make sense today. Saying this is to recognize the challenge of his conception to theologies that are satisfied with repeating past formulas. One cannot help being impressed by the sense of prophetic urgency that inspires him. The "method of correlation" of his systematic theology requires a permanent dialectic between man's quest and the answer of faith. It invites him to use a mass of material which most theologians would leave out of their directly theological endeavours: psychology, for instance, plays a dominant role in Tillich's expositions. Thus the Revelation makes sense, in his system, because it is the answer to "the finitude and ambiguities of actual reason";[85] the term God, as a symbol of the Unconditioned, is meaningful insofar as it resolves the contradictions of finite being; Christology itself answers the dilemma of existence and fulfils mankind's "quest for Christ."

The three parts of *Systematic Theology* that have been published so far are rooted in the spiritual needs of present-day society, which themselves interpret in our time the spiritual needs of man as such. The last volume of *Systematic Theology* will follow the same pattern. In Part IV, the theology of the Spirit will be presented as solving the riddle of life. Being, existence, life thus anticipate, in man's conscious and unconscious experience, the revelation of the Unconditioned as God, as Christ and as Spirit. In Part V, the notion of the Kingdom of God will resolve the ambiguities

82. *Ibid.*, p. 78.
84. *Ibid.*, p. 77.
83. *Ibid.*, p. 66.
85. *Systematic Theology* I, p. 81.

of history. The basic purpose of Tillich's theology is neither to establish facts, nor to build a speculative synthesis; it is to investigate meanings. Leaving the former task to positive theologians and their recurrent flirtation with historicism, and the latter to speculative theologians and the permanent danger of over-intellectualism, he opens another way, a search for the meanings of religious attitudes through a "critical phenomenology, uniting an intuitive-descriptive element with an existential-critical element."[86] However, by so doing, Tillich boldly heads for a third pitfall, which we may call a philosophical distortion of faith.

It is highly significant that the apparently far-reaching analyses of faith undertaken by Tillich end by disappointing the reader. The beautiful symphony concludes on a false note. I mean by this that there is not much point in the tremendous spiritual effort of all the religions of mankind if the only ultimately valid content of their faith is merely the intuition of a philosophical principle. Yet the meaning of faith, as drawn out of belief-ful experience by Paul Tillich, is simply that, in the depth of my own being, I participate in both abyss and ground, in nothingness and in being-itself. The difference between the philosopher and the faith-ful would be that the former is relatively detached whereas the latter is involved. If this is the meaning of faith and religion, we have obviously been let down by priests and prophets, and, what is more, we have been led astray. For neither priest nor prophet has taught that this was faith. To be sure, a certain amount of de-mythologizing is necessary—be it Primordial Man in India or Gilgamesch in Mesopotamia, myths have to be interpreted. The question is, is Tillich's method valid?

The contrast between the religious myths of faith and their reduction to one common philosophical denominator confirms what I have said elsewhere:[87] a philosophical description of being and concern is altogether distinct from a theology of faith and grace. Speaking in specifically Christian terms, it is a fallacy to

86. *Ibid.*, p. 107.
87. "Christianity and the Philosophies of Existence" (*Theological Studies*, March, 1957), pp. 10-12.

approach the faith of Christianity from a preconceived pheno-menological notion of faith at large. In the first place, this does not do justice to the fact that the Christian faith, in its Catholic form and also in its Protestant form before Schleiermacher, has always described itself, not as one faith among others, but as the only saving faith. Secondly, it introduces a distinction between the conveying message of faith (called, here, its myth or symbol) and its ultimate meaning. The Christian message, however, is essentially historical. Arising out of a historical event, the preach-ing of the man Jesus, it was confirmed by his Resurrection from the dead in Judea under the governor Pontius Pilate. The historical structure of the Christian faith stands in judgment over Tillich's analyses, for it implies that the form of the Christian Revelation is inseparable from its content. If it only expressed unconditional concern as a philosophical intuition of being and non-being, its historical structure would be altogether irrelevant to its meaning.

Actually it would be difficult to discover a systematic theology that appeals less to the historical sources of Christian doctrine than that of Tillich. What this implies for Christology proper will detain us later. It is enough now to note that the notion of faith, the notion of original sin, the notion of revelation, have been stripped by Tillich of their specifically Christian elements and made into universal philosophical concepts. One could heed Calvin's warning: "Should some mind, abandoning the wisdom contained in the Word of God, bring us a different doctrine, he must rightly be suspected of vanity and falsehood."[88] For a theologian to straitjacket the Christian faith in a scheme which is supposedly valid for all and sundry faiths is highly suspect.

At this stage, however, we should suspend judgment. Whatever the fallacy of his basic approach, Tillich may, in the development of his Christology, bring in the necessary corrections.

88. *Institutes*, Book I, ch. 9, n. 2.

Chapter IV

CHRISTOLOGY AS SYMBOL

AN outline of the Christology of Paul Tillich must in the first place take account of the levels of existence that Tillich distinguishes. Since Christology is the answer of the Christian Church to man's universal quest for the Unconditional, such an answer will be adapted to the several planes of human existence. From the point of view of theology there are several such levels, each providing a vantage-point from which one may look at the Christian answer. Each, in its sphere, is valid; and this validity is delimited by the scope of that sphere. This is to say that the Christian tradition has seen the rise of several Christologies or that Christology has developed several aspects and several formulas. These may, or may not, be contradictory. The important point is not to determine their absolute truth in the abstract, but their meaning in the concrete. One must perceive their relevance to the existence of man in its several depths.

The deepest level at which Christology may be studied is called by Tillich the "ontological awareness of the Unconditional." As we have seen, faith is basically, in the Tillichian world view, a pre-conceptual experience. As "the concern about our existence in its ultimate whence and whither,"[1] it precedes every formula of a solution and every formula of a search. "The faith which conquers sin by receiving reconciliation and a new being, must precede the search for ultimate reality."[2] If Christianity's claim to universality is valid, a Christian answer must be found at this level. Christology must be ontological. It must provide an answer at the very depth where the quest for the Unconditioned is ontologically pre-formulated. This ontological requirement corresponds to what Tillich calls "the ontological principle in the philosophy of

1. *Biblical Religion and the Search for Ultimate Reality*, p. 61.
2. *Ibid.*, pp. 55-56.

religion," and which he thus expresses: "Man is immediately aware of something unconditional which is the prius of separation and interaction of subject and object, theoretically as well as practically."[3] But we have to pass a hurdle here. At this level of existence, the implication cannot be directly formulated, it can only be pointed at. The Christian answer, like the answer of any religion, philosophy or revelation, will be *symbolic* and will be true only insofar as the symbol is grasped.

A second level of truth corresponds to the next plane of existence, that of history. Our experience is conditioned by historical circumstances. History has developed a culture which has profoundly influenced both our conscious thinking and our subconscious psyche. The Christian answer has precisely been couched in historical terms. Christ is presented as a historical person. This will therefore provide a second point of view: Christology as *historical*.

A third level of truth corresponds to the largely artificial distinction, in man, between his intellectual activity and other elements of his personality. In terms of beliefs, Christianity has been embodied in dogmas. These have an intellectual appeal and must be grasped rationally. We shall therefore study Christology as *dogmatic*.

Finally, another analysis of human behaviour sees man as an ethical being, whose convictions, principles and assumptions prompt him to adopt definite standards of conduct. Morality is not severed from assent. On the contrary, it expresses faith in the realm of ethical behaviour by cloaking the Christian answer in the garments of moral principles. A study of Christology should thus devote some time to Christology as *ethical*.

These points of view, or levels of truth, provide the structure of the four ensuing chapters. History, dogma and morality will be considered later. This chapter will be devoted to the symbolic framework of the Christian content of faith.

That Christian theology is symbolic follows upon the fact that it claims to be a formulation of faith. Faith, as man's attempt to

3. *Theology of Culture*, p. 22.

assert the Unconditional, cannot be expressed in conditioned language. But all language is conditioned. It is limited by the very concepts that it seeks to express, and by the linguistic tools at its disposal, which themselves result from long historical evolutions. To speak of formulating man's search for the Unconditional would therefore be to march towards a mirage, if there were no such thing as an indirect, symbolic use of language. And not only words are involved in this problem. Words correspond to concepts, which themselves depend on a previous or simultaneous experience of knowledge. Tillich's analysis of faith thus posits a fundamental critical problem concerning the structure of theological knowledge. As he has noted, "the centre of my theological doctrine of knowledge is the concept of symbol."[4]

We have already seen that a revelatory situation is revelatory insofar as it permits an awareness of the Unconditional as perceived through, underneath, and beyond the many elements that constitute the concrete situation. There is no revelation without a concrete setting. And a concrete setting is not revelatory unless it point beyond itself, to an eternal abyss, ground and meaning. This is to say that in the existential experience of the Unconditional, the human and cosmic elements, whose convergence have formed the situation in question, are perceived as symbolic of their eternal ground. The Unconditioned makes itself known through symbolic situations. In other words, it reaches us through symbols. The symbol belongs to the world of appearances. It may be a word, an image, a concept, a fact, a gesture, a person. It may be literally anything. For anything which has been involved in a concrete experience of the Unconditional may retain, for the mind which has known it in the fire of communion with being-itself, a flavour of remembrance. It has kept the power of reminding us of that experience. It has been endowed with a sort of secondary revelatory power; and whenever we meet this symbol, we shall be thrown back into the revelatory constellation that was once connected with this particular symbol. This is the main Tillichian use of the word symbol: it denotes the elements that have been associated with a revelation and that have retained

4. *The Theology of Paul Tillich*, p. 333.

some of the revelatory power then manifested. A second use of the term follows. We cannot speak of the Unconditional directly. Even to say "Unconditional" is to see it as contrasted with the conditional, and this conditions the content of the word "Unconditional." There is no way of expressing the ultimate ground of being unless we use symbolic terms. The terms are understood as pointers to, not as copies of, reality. God does not mean a God, but points to a reality that no language can circumscribe. Were the word "God" non-symbolic, it would be identical with "a God." But God is not a God. As Unconditional, he is beyond the realm where "a" is meaningful, beyond singular and plural; as Unconditional, he is neither subject of the verb "to be" nor object of the verb "to know," but he is beyond object and subject. "It is highly symbolic language which must be used at this point. But its symbolic character does not diminish its truth; on the contrary, it is a condition of its truth. To speak unsymbolically about being-itself falsifies the real situation."[5]

A number of problems are raised by this double use of symbols. In the first place, one may ask where the symbolic universe ends. Anything may be a symbol. But how do we know that what it points to is not itself a more abstract symbol? Paul Tillich admits that "in order to speak of symbolic knowledge one must delimit the symbolic realm by an unsymbolic statement."[6] Were there no limit to symbolism, there would be no knowledge either. Faith would imply an indefinite progress from symbol to further symbol, without any ultimate encounter with the Unsymbolic. That is, it would be a regress, an acknowledgement of the ultimacy of despair, of the impossibility of making sense out of the human situation, of the universal fallacy of thinking that revelatory situations truly are revelatory, of revelation without a content. Reacting to this criticism of some of his language, Tillich "became suspicious of any attempts to make the concept of symbol all-embracing and therefore meaningless."[7] What then is the unsymbolic statement that makes symbolic knowledge possible? It is "that God is being-itself and as such beyond the

5. *The Courage to Be*, p. 180.
6. *The Theology of Paul Tillich*, p. 334.   7. *Ibid.*

subject-object structure of everything that is."[8] It is interesting
to note that contrary to Tillich's impression, this is a beautiful
instance of symbolic language. The word "beyond" as applied
to the Unconditional is obviously a symbol, since it cannot have
a literal meaning unless God is the subject of this particular
statement. But if he is the subject of this statement, he is no longer
beyond the subject-object structure. What actually makes this
statement non-symbolic is not its form, which remains symbolic,
but the fact that it corresponds to an irreducible experience. A
symbol does not only point to something else; it also participates
in it. One should say that every statement about God is symbolic;
but one should add that, inasmuch as it is symbolic, it precisely
orients towards a non-symbolic reality immediately experienced.
This is confirmed by what Tillich writes in the second volume of
his *Systematic Theology*, and where he implicitly corrects himself.
Here, no statement is said to be non-symbolic. To say "that God
is the Infinite, or the Unconditional, or Being-itself" is no longer
presented as a non-symbolic statement. Rather, "these terms
precisely designate the boundary-line at which both the symbolic
and the non-symbolic coincide. Up to this point every statement
is non-symbolic (in the sense of religious symbol). Beyond this
point every statement is symbolic (in the sense of religious
symbol). The point itself is both symbolic and non-symbolic."[9]

A symbol is therefore not a mere sign. Paul Tillich strongly
insists on the difference between signs and symbols. A sign points
to a meaning with which it has no intrinsic connection. It is an
agreed, conventional way of saying something. Highway codes
are made of signs, not of symbols. A symbol on the contrary has
characteristics that distinguish it from a sign. In *Dynamics of Faith*,
Tillich lists four such marks. *First*, a symbol "participates in that
to which it points."[10] This is a consequence of the fact that it
became a symbol in the midst of a revelatory situation. Its association with revelation has lingered, and this makes it still participate
in the power of that which was revealed. The "beyond itself"
to which it points is no other than the revelation that was then
perceived. A *second* characteristic logically follows: "it opens up

8. *Ibid.*   9. *Systematic Theology* II, p. 10.   10. *Ibid.*, p. 42.

levels of reality which otherwise are closed for us,"[11] namely those levels to which we were raised in the original revelatory experience. *Thirdly*, it "not only opens up dimensions and elements of reality which otherwise remain unapproachable but also unlocks dimensions and elements of our soul which correspond to the dimensions and elements of reality."[12] A revelation would be unperceived, unless we had the capacity to perceive it. And only in the revelatory experience itself do we gauge the depths of our soul. What Tillich has called "ecstasy" corresponds to "miracle." The miracle is the correlation of elements having revelatory power. The ecstasy is the opening of the soul's depths to the depths of the situation.

Fourthly, "symbols cannot be produced intentionally."[13] In Tillich's theology, this is a principle of tremendous importance. That a symbol cannot be invented is evident, once it has been defined by its participation in a revelatory constellation. One does not create revelation, and only revelation creates symbols of itself. This is important for defining the function of theology. "Theology as such has neither the duty nor the power to confirm or to negate religious symbols. Its task is to interpret them according to theological principles and methods."[14] The theologian cannot discard traditional Christian symbols; that they are symbols and, as such, endowed with divine power, is enough for him. This cuts the ground from under much of liberal Protestantism and its rejection of Catholic symbols. Yet the theologian should criticize symbols: he "may discover contradictions between symbols."[15] He may also by his prophetic insight contribute to the surge of a new revelatory situation out of which new symbols will grow. This, for Tillich, condemns the "static" character which he attributes to Catholic sacramentalism and Catholic theology.

Fifthly, symbols, "like living beings, grow and die."[16] "They grow when the situation is ripe for them, and they die when the situation changes."[17] This seems a difficult point to accept. It

---

11. *Ibid.* 12. *Ibid.* 13. *Ibid.*, p. 43.
14. *Systematic Theology* I, p. 240. 15. *Ibid.*
16. *Dynamics of Faith*, p. 43. 17. *Ibid.*

creates no problem with respect to artistic or social symbols. With religious symbols, however, a question arises. If these develop from revelatory situations, the revelation that gave them birth will always be a revelation. One may conceive that after years have passed it may have lost some power, that people will no longer fully perceive in what way this particular situation was revelatory. But the fact will always remain that through these concrete symbols the Ultimate was once perceived. Tillich admits it: symbols that have become "latent" may be revived in favourable circumstances. Yet he maintains that religious symbols can undergo a "disintegration,"[18] losing their symbolic power.[19] This is a serious matter, for how can a symbol disintegrate if it truly partakes of the power of being-itself which it expresses? How can it fail to be revelatory, unless the reality of which it partakes also disintegrates?

When Tillich speaks of artistic symbols, he naturally does not encounter this problem. But when he speaks of the Unconditional as perceived in religion and faith, he does not seem to posit it with enough earnestness. He duly recognizes the difference between artistic and religious symbols. The latter "has special character in that it points to the ultimate level of being, to ultimate reality, to being itself, to meaning itself."[20] If this is admitted, how then can Tillich declare that when a religious symbol disintegrates, it means that the encounter with Ultimate reality out of which it grew has itself disintegrated? "They are the expression of an encounter with ultimate reality, and they disappear if this kind of encounter disappears."[21] Tillich rightly insists that "it is not theoretical criticism that kills religious symbols."[22] Theoretical refutation is powerless before the existential pregnancy of the symbol. But when he adds that symbols are killed by "a change in the actual encounter,"[23] one may ask how ultimate was the Ultimate that was perceived in that situation, if it can disappear? If the Unconditional is unconditional, it should be beyond the reach of the situation in which it was perceived. The situation

18. *The Protestant Era*, p. 62.
20. *The Religious Situation*, p. 109.
22. *Ibid.*

19. *Ibid.*, p. 63.
21. *Ibid.*, p. 111.
23. *Ibid.*

was a necessary, symbolic mediation for it to be perceived; but a person that has intuited the Unconditional knows it once for all, even after the various elements of the revelatory correlation have separated and lost their power. This leads to a basic criticism. If Tillich is right in connecting religious symbols and the Ultimate, he cannot be right in thinking that religious symbols die. For the Ultimate does not die. A symbol which is no longer made powerful by the existential context in which it became symbolic of Ultimate reality, remains symbolic of it by the very power of Ultimate reality already perceived. A symbol which has been truly symbolic of God is always symbolic of God. When it no longer leads to God, God comes to man through it. This would seem to be the conclusion logically to be drawn from Tillich's doctrine: "A symbol *has* truth: it is adequate to the revelation it expresses. A symbol *is* true: it is the expression of a true revelation."[24] Tillich fails to be consistent when he does not add: A symbol remains true as long as what it reveals is the truth. Since ultimate truth does not disintegrate, neither do its symbols. It is true that Tillich offers an explanation for the disintegration of religious symbols: "Religious symbols are double-edged. They are directed toward the infinite which they symbolize *and* toward the finite through which they symbolize it."[25] One can easily understand that "the symbol and, along with it, the reality from which it was taken" may disintegrate "in mutual interdependence."[26] Yet one cannot see why the Infinite lacks the power to maintain the symbolic relation even when the situation is no longer revelatory.

A last point concerning Tillich's conception of religious symbols should now be mentioned: a constellation of religious symbols forms what he calls a religious "myth."

"Myths are symbols of faith combined in stories about divine-human encounters."[27] One finds such myths in pagan religions, and they are present in the Old Testament and even in the New. In Tillich's usage, the word "myth" is not derogatory. Myths are as necessary as symbols. The correlation of several symbols even

24. *Systematic Theology* I, 240.   25. *Ibid.*
26. *The Protestant Era*, p. 63.   27. *Dynamics of Faith*, p. 49.

manifests an element of man's perception of the Unconditional which a symbol, by itself, would not convey, namely the historical and the cosmic relevance of the Unconditional. It "puts the stories of the gods into the framework of time and space."[28] In Tillich's view, this is legitimate if it expresses the transcendence of God above space and time. But it is radically ambiguous. Myths can contribute to unseat the Unconditional and to make man conceive of it as subject to time and space. This is why so many myths imply polytheism: myth "divides the divine into several figures, removing ultimacy from each of them without removing their claim to ultimacy."[29] Like symbols, therefore, myths must be criticized, and all great religions have done so. In modern times, and in the Christian context of the New Testament, this criticism has been given the name of de-mythologization, a matter which will claim our attention later. At this point it is enough to note that, for Tillich, myth and de-mythologization belong together, just like symbol and symbol-criticism. A myth which is not understood as symbolical but as literally true is a "pure myth." Its religious value is distorted by literalism. It is taken as a transcendent history of the life of God and of God's intervention in the life of man. Such myths must be broken. Only a "broken myth"[30] has undoubted religious value, precisely because its value has resisted the radical criticism of de-mythologization. But the criticism of myth should bear on the real, not on the imagined shortcomings of the mythical story. Pagan mythology has often been criticized for its supposed immorality, yet, as Tillich rightly points out, "these attacks are only partially justified. The relations of the mythological gods are trans-moral; they are ontological; they refer to structures of being and to conflicts of values."[31]

The only ultimately valid criticism of a myth must take account of the religious dimension of the myth. It must be seen as an attempt to perceive and express the concept that God is living and the experience of man faced with the fascinating mystery of the holiness of God's life. Because it is made of symbols that are

28. *Ibid.*
30. *Ibid.*, p. 50.
29. *Ibid.*
31. *Systematic Theology* I, 224.

themselves the products of a series of revelatory situations, a myth may be successfully criticized only from within its own revelatory context. This is what Tillich calls the "theological circle." Only the Unconditional which the myth wants to express can judge the myth. Only in its light can the myth be considered inadequate, misleading or, perhaps, fallacious. In the light of the Ultimate, however, all myths are ambiguous. For if they combine symbols, that is, revelatory situations, the system into which these are united is not itself a revelatory situation. It is, precisely, a myth, arising out of religious imagination. Because of this bipolarity—combining genuine revelatory situations into imaginative patterns—myths must be neither destroyed, negated, nor accepted in their literalism. They must be "broken," understood on the level of the ultimate dimension of existence, which they depict in ambiguous traits and colours.

"Christianity was born, not with the birth of the man who is called Jesus, but in the moment in which one of his followers was driven to say to him, 'Thou art the Christ.' "[32] The cornerstone of Tillich's Christology is that the revelation carried by Jesus must have been known in a revelatory situation. This implies the convergence of a "miraculous," power-revealing situation, and of someone grasping the meaning of this situation in an ecstasy of faith. The most striking such moment, as recorded in the New Testament, is the confession of Peter professing his faith that "Thou art the Christ." The problem of the man Jesus will concern us when we study the historical aspects of Tillich's Christology. Now we will concentrate on the meaning of the confession "Thou art the Christ." For the term "Christ" is evidently the central symbol of Christology. It is in the light of it that every other symbol is meaningful and that every Christian assertion about Jesus must be criticized. In the light of it, too, Christians will judge the attempts of other religions to identify the Christ differently from what Christianity asserts. With the symbol of the Christ we are at the cosmic crossroads of all religions.

32. *Ibid.*, II, p. 97.

For, as the analysis of faith has shown, all religions try to identify the depths of man; they endeavour to find the name of the ground of being. The concrete content of a religious faith is an equation of being-itself with the meaning of a religious symbol or myth. The essential content of every religious faith, whatever the concrete content involved, is that in the depths of man is experienced the ultimate ground of all being, the Unconditional. The term Christ, in Christianity, gives a name to the Unconditional, the eternal ground of all that is. But it is more than a name; it is an identification with an event of history. There has been a man in whom "Essential Godmanhood has appeared within existence and subjected itself to the conditions of existence without being conquered by them."[33] By Essential Godmanhood Tillich means the eternal ground of man. The analysis of man's existential estrangement, which classical theology calls original sin, shows that by the very fact of his existence, man has fallen from his essential being to an existential situation. The essential being of man corresponds exactly to his point of contact with the Absolute. It is not only manhood as experienced in existence, but it is also manhood as created in God, ontologically before the fall into existence. This Tillich calls Godmanhood. Essential Godmanhood is thus the being of man prior to existence. It is man in God. "To essential man belongs the unity of his finiteness with his infinity, and it is precisely this unity which I call Godmanhood, because it is an expression of the dialectical interdependence of finiteness and infinity."[34]

Christianity claims that this Essential Godmanhood has, in a concrete event and a concrete man, appeared within the conditions of existence, inside the weft of history, without falling from essence and without being distorted by the ebb and flow of existence. In Christ "Eternal Godmanhood"[35] has been seen. When it was seen Jesus was known as the Christ, the expectation of mankind finally fulfilled, the One who brings in the new eon, the New

33. *Ibid.*, p. 98.
34. "A Reinterpretation of the Doctrine of the Incarnation," in *Church Quarterly Review* (London, England), No. 294, Jan.-March, 1949, p. 143.
35. *Systematic Theology* II, p. 100.

Being. Because he was thus perceived, Tillich may say: "Jesus is the Christ for us."[36] And because the Christ means Essential Godmanhood, he may add: "The Christ is God-for-us."[37] Jesus would not have been the Christ, and, as the Christ, he would not have been the manifestation of Eternal Godmanhood, if manhood had not acknowledged him. For there is no revelatory situation without the ecstasy of recognition in which one discovers a manifestation of being-itself.

The symbol of the Christ, therefore, which is borrowed from the Jewish conception of the Messiah, or King, or Anointed, can easily be distorted. Jesus as the Christ must not "be seen as a God walking on earth,"[38] as "a divine-human automaton without serious temptation, real struggle, or tragic involvement in the ambiguities of life."[39] This would be a misunderstood myth. It could not be the manifestation of a reality in which one partakes. It would not be the revelation of the ground of being. Caught in existential estrangement, man could not grasp the meaning of a divine-human avatar. A human being named Jesus who would not be subject to the involvements of existence could not be revelatory since man could not step into the non-existential theological circle where he would make sense. On the contrary, the Christ has been known, "touched with our hands, seen with our eyes." And he has been known, not only as a man named Jesus, but as "Jesus who is called the Christ".[40] This means that in Jesus we have "the picture of a personal life which is subjected to all the consequences of existential estrangement but wherein existential estrangement is conquered in himself and a permanent unity is kept with God."[41] The ground of being, which we only perceive in hope, to which we are unconditionally committed without the evidence that we are in contact with it, dominated the ambiguities of existence in the Christ. Under its power, the Christ did not undergo "original sin"; his existence did not imply a fall: it maintained in its integrality the dominion of Essential Godmanhood over the tragedies of life.

36. *Ibid.*, p. 101.
37. *Ibid.*, p. 100.
38. *Ibid.*, p. 133.
39. *Ibid.*, p. 135.
40. *Ibid.*, p. 98.
41. *Ibid.*, p. 135.

The universal quest of mankind has been fo' this return to unity, for this recovery of the ground of being which supports us and from which we are estranged. To perceive it in the Christ is to hear the good news that "the Christ is the one who brings in the new eon," to expect "the coming of a new state of things through him,"[42] the state of things in which we ourselves have recovered Essential Godmanhood and have risen from the state of estrangement to that of reunion with being-itself. Tillich uses the symbol "New Being" to point to this. Man's quest has been for a New Being that would conquer the dichotomy between subject and object. "New Being is essential being under the conditions of existence, conquering the gap between essence and existence."[43] This symbol itself can be misread. The Being which is manifested in the Christ is new indeed, but not in the sense that it has done away with the circumstances of estrangement that mark existential being. Tragedy is still there, but henceforth it has been conquered. It is there, but no longer as victorious. "The New Being is new insofar as it is the undistorted manifestation of essential being within and under the conditions of existence. It is new in two respects: it is new in contrast to the merely potential character of essential being; and it is new over against the estranged character of existential being."[44] In the Christ alone, man's relation to the ground of being is fully actual and fully un-distorted. In ourselves, subject as we are to existential estrangement, Godmanhood is only potential; it is a state of dreaming innocence in which we never were and from which, speaking symbolically, we fell when we came into being. Our actual being is divorced from it, and the constant dream of man has been for a return to the beginning, a restoration of that which has been lost because we never had it, innocence, essence, Godmanhood. This is the New Being we long for. In Christ it has been mani-fested. Essential being has come to existence without distortion. Innocence has become experience without losing its pristine virginity. Estrangement has been conquered. "The New Being has appeared in a personal life."[45] Tillich's formula for the

42. *Ibid.*, p. 118.   43. *Ibid.*, p. 119.
44. *Ibid.*   45. *Ibid.*, p. 120.

Christian message is this: "We want to communicate to you an experience we have had that here and there in the world and now and then in ourselves is a New Creation, usually hidden, but sometimes manifest, and certainly manifest in Jesus who is called the Christ."[46] Out of their participation in the revelatory situation in which Jesus is perceived to be the Christ, Christians witness to the vision they have had of the New Reality, which is "reconciliation, reunion, resurrection . . . the New Creation, the New Being, the New state of things."[47]

Tillich insists that "Jesus as the Christ is the bearer of the New Being in the totality of his being, not in any special expressions of it."[48] Various Christologies have concentrated on his words, his deeds or his suffering. These are enlightening if not cut off from the being of Christ. But rationalism separated his words, pietism his deeds, and orthodoxy his suffering from his being; these systems forgot "that the being of Christ is his work and that his work is his being, namely, the New Being which is his being."[49] When theologians overlook the being of Christ they cannot place the New Being at the centre of their thought. Concentrating on his acts, they unavoidably distort their meaning and relevance. They then no longer relate the Christ to the universal quest for a conquest of estrangement. This makes the Christ himself a stranger in mankind.

On the contrary, we should remember that the traditional symbols of "salvation," "redemption," "grace," "atonement," "mediation" as applied to the function of the Christ, emphasize the universality of his role. The New Being in the Christ has universal significance. It is universally expected. On account of this, "Jesus as the Christ is the Saviour through the universal significance of his being as the New Being."[50] What is this significance? Simply that the revelatory correlation in which Peter acknowledged his Messiahship remains revelatory for every man. While Peter was directly thrown into it, being face to face with the Christ in the flesh, we are in a different position. It is the same

46. *The New Being*, p. 18.   47. *Ibid.*, p. 24.
48. *Systematic Theology* II, p. 121.   49. *Ibid.*, p. 168.
50. *Ibid.*, p. 169.

situation, but the participants in it are removed from it in time and space. "The original miracle, together with its original reception, is the permanent point of reference, while the spiritual reception by following generations changes continuously."[51] A whole ecclesiology is evidently implied in this statement. The Church will be the community in which one experiences the original revelatory correlation in which Jesus was acknowledged as the Christ. The main point here is that this revelatory constellation has universal scope. In this sense it is "final," not that no more revelations may take place, but that all other revelations will be subordinated to it.

> The revelatory event is Jesus as the Christ. He is the miracle of the final revelation, and his reception is the ecstasy of the final revelation. His appearance is the decisive constellation of historical (and by participation, natural) forces. It is the ecstatic moment of human history and, therefore, its centre, giving meaning to all possible and actual history. . . . But it is only for those who received him as the final revelation, namely, as the Messiah, the Christ, the Man-from-above, the Son of God, the Spirit, the Logos-who-became-flesh, the New Being.[51a]

Because the New Being has universal scope and reaches all men in a revelatory constellation, it is "valid for mankind as such."[52] Can we go further and extend the universality of the New Being in the Christ to the entire cosmos? In the first volume of *Systematic Theology*, Tillich answers affirmatively: "In an indescribable way, it has meaning for the universe also. Nothing less than this should be asserted by Christian theology."[53] In the second volume, however, the universality of the Christ has somehow been bound to the limits of "historical mankind."[54] "Our basic answer leaves the universe open for possible divine manifestations in other areas or periods of being. Such possibilities cannot be denied. But they cannot be proved or disproved. Incarnation is unique for the special group in which it happens, but it is not unique in the

51. *Ibid.*, I, p. 126.   51a. *Ibid.*, I, p. 136.
52. *Ibid.*, p. 137.   53. *Ibid.*
54. *Ibid.*, II, p. 95.

sense that other singular incarnations for other unique worlds are excluded."[55] If there are such other revelations in other spaces, we do not know. Yet the manifestation of the New Being in one place suggests that the New Being manifests itself wherever estrangement has to be conquered. "Otherwise self-destruction would be the inescapable consequence."[56]

One should examine the implications of the symbols of Christ and of New Being as far as the formulation of faith is concerned. Certainly traditional Christology has not expressed the meaning of Christ as Tillich does. His basic point, that Christ is the historical manifestation of Eternal Godmanhood, is filled with implications. All Christian dogmas, both in their Catholic form and in the form that was classical in Orthodox Protestantism, must be radically reinterpreted in the light of Tillich's interpretation of the basic Christian symbols. This all-important question may be shelved, however, until Tillich has given us more insights into his thought. The problems raised by his explanation of symbolic Christology are twofold. In the first place, we should ascertain to what extent history backs up his interpretation, and, in the second, confront his world-view with the traditional Christian dogmas. What is the status of history in symbolic Christology? And what is the dogmatic meaning of the same Christology?

In particular, can Essential Godmanhood, as manifested in the Christ, be identified with God? The classical dogma has called the Christ God. Does Tillich's Christology permit such an identification? This will be the centre of the dogmatic problem as we shall have to examine it. Before being able to answer these questions, we should unfold some of Tillich's interpretations of other Christian symbols. Christ and the New Being are no doubt fundamental, yet they are not alone. Other aspects have to be pointed to by means of other symbols. One of these brings us to the brink of the dogmatic question of the divinity of Christ. It is the symbol of Christ as the Logos or Word of God. "Jesus as the Christ is the Logos."[57] Such a statement, in Tillich's language,

55. *Ibid.*, p. 96.   56. *Ibid.*
57. *Ibid.*, p. 57.

is "paradoxical." That is, it "contradicts the *doxa*, the opinion derived from man's existential predicament and all expectations imaginable on the basis of this predicament."[58] This opinion formulates the universal fact of estrangement. The paradox is that a human being, living under the conditions of estrangement, nevertheless conquered and dominated them. One should not examine this from the standpoint of logic, but from that of experience: "The paradox is a new reality and not a logical riddle."[59] Statements concerning the Christ are not therefore to be justified on the level of philosophical logic. They stand or fall on the strength of the revelatory situation which imposes them, which is all the more remarkable since "Logos" and "Word" are of philosophical origin and have philosophical connotations.

The doctrine of the Word of God has been obscured by the various meanings which Christianity has attributed to the expression. Tillich distinguishes six. (1) The first meaning is the closest to its philosophical origin. The Word, or Logos, "is first of all the principle of the divine self-manifestation in the ground of being itself. The ground is not only an abyss in which every form disappears; it also is the source from which every form emerges. The ground of being has the character of self-manifestation; it has *logos* character. This is not something added to the divine life; it is the divine life itself."[60] Other meanings of the term Word are derivative. The Word is (2) "the medium of creation, the dynamic spiritual world which mediates between the silent mystery of the abyss of being and the fullness of concrete, individualized, self-related beings";[61] (3) "the manifestation of the divine life in the history of revelation"; (4) "the manifestation of the divine life in the final revelation"; (5) "the document of the final revelation"; (6) "the message of the Church as proclaimed in her preaching and teaching."[62]

The important element in Tillich's Christology is that the first, second, third and fourth meanings of the term Word all coincide in the event of Jesus as the Christ. This is to say that the Christ

---

58. *Ibid.*, p. 92.
59. *Ibid.*
60. *Ibid.*, I, pp. 157-58.
61. *Ibid.*, p. 158.
62. *Ibid.*, p. 159.

is the New Being able to conquer the situation of estrangement because he is primordially "the principle of the divine self-manifestation." That which appeared in the history of mankind in the shape of Jesus and which was recognized as the New Being by the Apostles is no other than the very abyss and ground of everything that is. The symbol of the Word, in itself, can be detached from a historical manifestation. It could be the self-manifestation of God, the demonstration of being-itself to being-itself, the infinite depth and wisdom of the divine. It is all this, and also something more: the manifestation of being-itself in one concrete human being, Jesus. This is borne out by applying the symbol of "the Word of God" to the Christ.

At this point, the symbol of the Word interlocks with Trinitarian thinking. The Word is the Word of God, the self-manifestation of the divine life, not an added achievement of it, but the divine life as such. That God may be called, not only God, but also Word, is one of the bases of Trinitarian theology. We should therefore examine, with Paul Tillich, the meaning of the Trinitarian symbols. The doctrine of the Christ dovetails into a doctrine of God and, more specifically, of God as Three. Tillich recognizes this when he writes: "The doctrine of revelation is based on a Trinitarian interpretation of the divine life and its self-manifestation."[63]

The problem of the Trinity as the divine life prior to a knowledge of the Christ is frequently discussed in Tillich's works. The Trinity is a symbol which ontological reflection elaborates. It points towards a basic implication of being-itself, when being-itself is understood not as a static background to the universe, but as the live ground from which all stems. Being-itself is life. It is pregnant with all the forms that have come out in time. But since it is being-itself, the ground, the mother or the womb of all, it cannot be dependent on what will be born of it. Being-itself is living even before concrete forms have come to be. When we say "before," we naturally speak symbolically. But this symbol of anteriority is necessary. It expresses the traditional doctrine that

63. *Ibid.*, p. 157.

God is Creator even before creation. His life does not depend on his works. He is life. Thus "the idea of the living God requires a distinction between the abysmal element of the divine, the form element, and their spiritual unity."[64] Since life is not static, we may establish a symbolic distinction between the divine abyss out of which the life of God manifests itself, the self-manifestation of this life and, thirdly, the unity of the two. The abyss is a pole of ultimacy; the form a pole of concreteness. And both are one. "The Trinitarian problem is the problem of the unity between ultimacy and concreteness in the living God."[65] Tillich shows that each type of monotheistic religion, since it has conceived of God as living, has developed a form of Trinitarian thinking. "Monarchical" monotheism saw life emanating from the highest God in a multitude of incarnations and demi-gods. "Mystical" monotheism was Trinitarian in developing "the relation of the Brahman-Atman, the absolute, to the concrete gods of Hindu piety."[66] Finally, the "exclusive" monotheism of the Bible made room for the element of mediation in the divine life, and there arose mediating figures, which Tillich classifies in three groups: first "hypostatized divine qualities, like Wisdom, Word, Glory"; second, "divine messengers"; third, "the divine-human figure through whom God works the fulfilment of history, the Messiah."[67] In the fully developed Christian thinking, the three elements of life, fathomless abyss, sprouting ground, and the unity of the two, are called Father, Son, Spirit. A beautiful page of *Systematic Theology* I shows the interrelatedness of the three. The first principle is "that which makes God, God. It is the root of his majesty, the unapproachable intensity of his being, the inexhaustible ground of being."[68] This is God in terms of power to be. The second principle is the *logos*; it is "the mirror of the divine depth, the principle of God's self-objectivization"; it "opens the divine ground, its infinity and its darkness, and it makes its fullness distinguishable, definite, finite."[69] This is God in terms of "meaning and structure."[70] Finally, the third principle,

64. *Ibid.*, II, p. 143.   65. *Ibid.*, I, p. 228.
66. *Ibid.*, p. 229.   67. *Ibid.*   68. *Ibid.*, p. 250.
69. *Ibid.*, p. 251.   70. *Ibid.*

or Spirit, is "the actualization of the other two." It ensures that God remains God, in that the *logos*-process of definite structuring returns to its infinite ground: "The finite is posited as finite within the process of divine life, but it is reunited with the infinite within the same process."[71]

Paul Tillich takes a dim view of the sort of theology that sees in the Trinity a numerical problem. Luther "rejected a theology which makes the Trinitarian dialectic into a play with meaningless number combinations."[72] In this he was right. For "the trinitarian problem has nothing to do with the trick question how one can be three and three be one."[73] If it is treated as a matter for abstract speculation, it becomes a meaningless juggling with words and numbers. Forgotten is the fact that Trinitarian terms like Father, Son, Spirit, or, in the traditional nomenclature, *personae*, relations, processions, generation, spiration, are symbols pointing to aspects of being-itself as living. Making them objects that somehow have to be reconciled in spite of the fact that they are contradictory misses the entire meaning of Trinitarian thinking. The theology of the life of God becomes an attempt to square the circle, to make one into three and three into one. Instead, Trinitarian theology must be dialectical. As such, it is not a speculation on the incomprehensible or the absurd, but on all life. "Dialectics determine all life-processes and must be applied in biology, psychology and sociology. The description of tensions in living organisms, neurotic conflicts and class struggles, is dialectical. Life itself is dialectical."[74] From this existential basis, Trinitarian thought applies dialectics to the life of God, and makes it a symbol of Infinite Life. "If applied symbolically to the divine life, God as a living God must be described in dialectical statements. He has the character of all life, namely, to go beyond himself and to return to himself."[75] The meaning of these symbols, therefore, does not derive from logical speculation on numbers or philosophical speculation on the categories. Their meaning arises out of the revelatory situation in which all life appears as par-

71. *Ibid.*
73. *Ibid.*, I, p. 228.
75. *Ibid.*

72. *Ibid.*, II, p. 144.
74. *Ibid.*, II, p. 90.

taking of the pattern of divine life; it is inseparable from the experience of life. "The Trinitarian symbols become empty if they are separated from their two experiential roots—the experience of the living God and the experience of the New Being in the Christ."[76]

So far, Trinitarian theology has been dealt with independently of Christology. Yet Tillich is quite aware that, in the history of Christianity, Christology was primary. The "experience of the New Being in Christ" prompted the definition of a Trinitarian dogma. The revelatory constellation in which Jesus was known as the Christ coincided with the revelatory situation in which life is experienced as power, ground and unity.

In an ecstasy which went deeper than ever into the event of the Christian revelation, Jesus as the Christ was identified with the second principle of divine life, with the pregnant womb of all forms, with "the creative ground of the finite," who "eternally produces the finite potentialities in himself."[77] Thus the experience of the New Being determined the form that Trinitarian thinking would take in Christianity. It prompted Christians to define the Christ as the *Logos* of Trinitarian theology. The "decisive element of the relation of the Christ to the Logos"[78] became part of Christology. The universal Trinitarian intuition encountered the experience of the New Being and furnished it with new symbols. Christology was thenceforth expressed in Trinitarian symbols. The Christ was not only the Messiah, the Mediator, the Son of Man; he was also the Son of God, the Word of God.

What this entails in terms of dogma we shall leave for later consideration. We are now analysing Tillich's conception of the Trinity as a symbol of God's life. That the Christ is one of the Trinity is a symbol. It means that the New Being which, in Christ, subjected itself to the conditions of existence without being destroyed by them, is being-itself, the ground of all. The event of Jesus as the Christ has universal significance, not because of any universal mission conferred on him arbitrarily, but because the Christ is the rich, inexhaustible source of all life. He is Being

76. *Ibid.*, pp. 143-44.   77. *Ibid.*, p. 91.
78. *Ibid.*, p. 143.

as ever New. Beyond object and subject, beyond essence and existence, he breathes all essences out of his infinite ground and he calls them back to himself in their finite existential forms. Experiencing in the flesh the conditions of estrangement which are man's daily bread, he overcomes and "saves" them by relating them to their eternal ground. He is the focal point of all existence and life, the Christ, the New Being, the second principle of the divine Life.

The symbols that point to the New Being as manifested in the personal life of Jesus may be misunderstood. They actually have been, whenever man's hunger for spiritual security has led him to distort the nature of the New Being. It is especially the Catholic temptation to picture the New Creation as the introduction into the world of a new institution. Shelter-like, the Church offers protection against the disintegrating forces of the world. She staves off false philosophies and leads the good fight for the law and the rights of God. She has assembled a whole arsenal of protective devices with powerful psychological impact. This, as seen by Paul Tillich, is her tragedy. The "mechanizing of her hierarchial apparatus"[79] was to be expected, for she overlooked an important aspect of Christology, which it would be the vocation of Protestantism to restore. It has been traditional in Lutheranism to present Luther's theology as a *theologia crucis*, as distinguished from the *theologia gloriae* of Catholicism. Christianity is a theology of the Cross. The Christ did indeed appear in glory; but nowhere was his glory seen more directly than on the Cross. In Tillich's categories, the proclamation of the Cross forms the essence of the Protestant principle. "Protestantism must proclaim the judgment that brings assurance by depriving us of all security; the judgment that declares us whole in the disintegration and cleavage of soul and community; the judgment that affirms our having truth in the very absence of truth (even of religious truth); the judgment that reveals the meaning of our life in the situation in which all the meaning of life has disappeared."[80]

The New Being that is perceived in Jesus as the Christ and of

79. *The Protestant Era,* p. 195.   80. *Ibid.,* p. 204.

which we catch an obscure glimpse whenever, in the ecstasy of a revelatory situation, we are infinitely concerned, is new because it is old. It is as old as being-itself, transcending time and space, having been before anything concrete was. It is the second principle of the Trinitarian life of God. But it is known nowhere by man except in the estranged situation which is the stuff of existence; it is perceived only "in the radical experience of the boundary-situation."[81] In the story of Christ, this insight is expressed in the symbol of the Cross: the Christ, who dominates existence, yet slaves under its harsh conditions. "The first relation of the Christ to existence is his subjection to it. . . . The subjection to existence is expressed in the symbol of the Cross of the Christ."[82] It is not complete and final, being correlated to the conquest of existence and its symbol, the Resurrection. It is nevertheless central. A Christology which would not see that the manifestation of the New Being takes place nowhere but in a boundary-situation would miss the main point of Christianity. The interdependence of the Cross and the Resurrection, of defeat and victory, gives universal relevance to an otherwise sad story. "The Cross of the Christ is the Cross of the one who has conquered the death of existential estrangement. Otherwise it would only be one more tragic event (which it *also* is) in the long history of the tragedy of man."[83] It also constitutes the unique contribution of Christianity to a philosophy of religion. In general religions have worshipped God as "Lord and Father"; they have adored him as Creator and Judge. Hence they have organized priestly castes for mediation, and hence they have provoked prophetic protests: "the Lord who is only Lord" and "the Father who is only Father"[84] "cannot be man's ultimate concern."[85] For besides reverence and sentimental love, such religions also inspire revolt and contempt. Christianity alone has conceived of "the manifestation of the Lord and Father as Son and Brother under the conditions of existence."[86] The conditions of existence mean tragedy. They make failure inseparable from effort,

81. *Ibid.*, p. 203.   82. *Systematic Theology* II, pp. 152-53.
83. *Ibid.*, p. 153.   84. *Ibid.*, I, p. 288.
85. *Ibid.*   86. *Ibid.*, p. 289.

stumbling necessary in the search for an ideal. He who is the Christ was doomed. He had to meet his fate on the Cross.

Christianity centres on the Cross, with its "universal symbolic significance." The story of the Cross "is the myth of the bearer of the new eon who suffers the death of a convict and slave under the powers of that old eon which he is to conquer."[87] The faith of Christianity expresses the meaning of this symbol: "the surrender of him who is called the Christ to the ultimate consequence of existence, namely, death under the conditions of estrangement."[88] The symbolic meaning of the Cross has many aspects.

In terms of life, the Cross points to the insight that the new life cannot be superadded to the old. "The new life would not really be new life if it did not come from the complete end of the old life. Otherwise it would have to be buried again. But if the new life has come out of the grave, then the Messiah himself has appeared."[89] In Tillich's view, Christian theology is not a "supra-naturalism" whereby something is added to nature as a result of an heteronomous decision. Rather, it is "self-transcending"[90] through self-sacrifice. It teaches the redemption of nature through the negation of nature. In this way the Cross becomes the pattern for faith and theology. In the symbol of the Cross the Christ "stands the double test of finality: uninterrupted unity with the ground of his being and the continuous sacrifice of himself as Jesus to himself as the Christ."[91]

In terms of Godmanhood, the Cross is a symbol "of the divine paradox of the appearance of the eternal God-man unity within existential estrangement."[92] Nowhere else should we look for the power and the glory, not in the birth of Jesus, not in the transfiguration, not in the miracles, not in the preaching of the beatitudes, not in the Resurrection—unless all these are seen as leading to, or flowing from, the "paradox of the Cross, that God is present in an actual human body and that it is just in suffering that his majesty is revealed."[93] The Cross is by no means the only

87. *Ibid.*, II, pp. 153-54.   88. *Ibid.*, p. 155.
89. *The Shaking of the Foundations*, p. 168.
90. *Systematic Theology* II, pp. 6 ff.   91. *Ibid.*, I, p. 170.
92. *Ibid.*, II, p. 159.   93. *The Religious Situation*, p. 170.

symbol of the manifestation of the ground of being. Yet "it is the central one, the criterion of all other manifestations of God's participation in the suffering of the world."[94]

In terms of Protestantism, the Cross is the ultimate symbol of the Protestant principle: what takes place at the Cross is the same as what happens, according to Tillich, wherever true Protestantism is to be found: "In the power of the New Being, the boundary-situation is preached, its No and Yes are proclaimed."[95] This is the acted event of justification by faith. The Christ dying is also resurrecting, thus revealing his unity with the New Being. "No longer is the universe subjected to the law of life out of birth. It is subjected to a higher law, to the law of life out of death by the death of him who represented eternal life."[96] The Protestant principle of the justification of him who is unjust is a Yes and a No: No to oneself and Yes to oneself. No alone would entail despair, and Yes alone would breed arrogance. In Christians both Yes and No are true, because when they say "Amen through Christ," they express their ultimate certitude: "There is no ultimate certitude except the life which has conquered its death and the truth which has conquered its error, the Yes which is beyond Yes and No."[97] The message of the Cross is that Jesus as the Christ is the only reality "where there is not Yes and No, but only Yes."[98]

Paul Tillich is eloquent when he unveils the symbolism of the Cross. One can only admire his reverence for the mystery which is revealed and the depth which he sees in it. And one can hardly resist quoting him at length again and again. Yet one feels a certain embarrassment: at times Tillich gives the impression of having discovered the fullness of the symbol of the Cross all by himself. He praises the Fathers who composed the Apostles' Creed for the fact that one of its great features "is that in the all-embracing second article it has enumerated symbols of subjection along with symbols of victory."[99] Credit should therefore be

94. *Systematic Theology* II, p. 175.   95. *The Protestant Era*, p. 205.
96. *The New Being*, p. 178.   97. *Ibid.*, p. 103.
98. *Ibid.*   99. *Systematic Theology* II, p. 159.

given to them for reading the symbolism of the Cross and confessing its relevance to Christian faith. But this is not what Tillich
does. He sees in their confession only an anticipation: they
"anticipated the basic structure in which the universal significance
of Jesus the Christ as the bearer of the New Being must be
seen."[100] Who fulfilled the anticipation we are left to imagine.

One thing is certain. For Tillich, the anticipation was not
fulfilled by Catholicism. Catholicism may be great. "Whenever
the hardness and crust are broken through and the substance
becomes visible, it exercises a peculiar fascination; then we see
what was once the life-substance and the inheritance of us all
and what we have now lost, and a deep yearning awakens in us
for the departed youth of our culture."[101] But Catholicism is
"consistently heteronomous."[102] Refusing to place itself under
judgment, it implicitly rejects the Cross. It has abandoned the
prophetic spirit which says "no" together with "yes" and "yes"
together with "no." "Ecclesiastically limited Catholicism,
petrified and mechanized in its forms,"[103] is unable to place itself
on the Cross and, through repentance and self-condemnation,
to give itself a new life. Just as "Jesus could not have been the
Christ without sacrificing himself as Jesus to himself as the
Christ,"[104] so must a Church sacrifice itself. "The criterion of the
truth of faith is that it implies an element of self-negation."[105]
Catholicism professes no such element. "Driven by this criterion,
Protestantism has criticized the Roman Church."[106] This Church
has been led into forms of idolatry because she did not take
seriously enough the Cross of the Christ.

Only in Protestantism has the Cross been given its due place.
Protestantism is not only a protest. "It is also—and above all—
Christianity. It is also and above all the bearer and mediator of
the 'New Being' manifest in Jesus as the Christ."[107] Protestantism
is thus found wherever—even outside of Protestant denomina-
tions, even outside of professedly Christian groups—the boun-

100. *Ibid.*
102. *Ibid.*
104. *Dynamics of Faith*, pp. 97-98.
106. *Ibid.*, p. 98.
101. *The Protestant Era*, p. 194.
103. *The Religious Situation*, p. 188.
105. *Ibid.*, p. 97.
107. *The Protestant Era*, p. 195.

dary-situation is proclaimed to be the very situation of salvation; wherever the meaning of the Cross is announced; wherever "the Christian substance"[108] is preached under the shadow of the Cross. "The fact that this criterion is identical with the Protestant principle and has become reality in the Cross of the Christ constitutes the superiority of Protestant Christianity."[109]

Yet not all Protestantism is thus saved. The "end of the Protestant era" means precisely that institutional Protestantism is no longer the standard-bearer of the Protestant principle. It "is merely on the defensive."[110] If the "protest against itself on the basis of an experience of God's majesty constitutes the Protestant principle,"[111] it is evident that the Churches are not engaged in protesting against themselves. The basic problem of Protestant institutions is to elaborate positive forms of life while constantly denying their sufficiency. This is so difficult that Tillich's objection to institutionalism may be turned against him. If to institutionalize salvation often entails a withdrawal of the element of self-negation, an undermining of the meaning of the Cross, is not Tillich himself transcending self-negation when he proclaims "the superiority of Protestant Christianity"? This pride in superiority is as arrogant as the "sacramental authority"[112] of bishops and priests has ever been. If a claim to superiority is clearly justified, a moderate pride in it may be forgiven. Yet how Protestant is Protestantism? The institutional Churches being partly discarded, what remains? There remain those who are, according to Tillich's standards, Protestant unawares. "Where are the Protestants?"[113] They are wherever Protestantism appears "as the prophetic spirit which lists where it will, without ecclesiastical conditions, organization and tradition. Thus it will operate through Catholicism as well as through orthodoxy, through freedom as well as through communism."[114] The question is, Are the Reformers themselves among these disciples of the ground of being? It is by fidelity to the Cross that, according to Tillich,

108. *Ibid.*, p. 196.
110. *The Protestant Era*, p. 229.
112. *Ibid.*, p. 227.
114. *Ibid.*, p. 232.

109. *Dynamics of Faith*, p. 98.
111. *Ibid.*, p. 226.
113. *The Protestant Era*, p. 231.

the God of Protestantism "has no sacraments which can be divorced from the prophetic message and therefore no priesthood and no genuine cult."[115] Two comments are pertinent. In the first place, how can Christian faith involve a true relation to God if it does not inspire adoration? And adoration means cult. In the second place, it has always been the Christian understanding of the Cross that the Cross was an expression, a symbol, of worship. This is why the Church Fathers saw in it the unique sacrifice of the Son of God. Catholicism has embodied this in its theology of the Eucharist, which is a re-presentation of the unique sacrifice of the Cross, of the cult offered by Jesus the Christ to the Father. The Reformers strenuously maintained that, in the words of the Confession of Augsburg, "the Passion of Christ was an oblation and a satisfaction."[116] That is, it was an act of divine cult. On this transcendent meaning of the Cross, Paul Tillich is silent.

Once more, Tillich has been caught in the snare of ontology. He has ontologized the symbol of the Cross. The term "sacrifice" now means "sacrifice of himself as Jesus to himself as the Christ," that is, sacrifice of the individual Jesus to the ground of being in him. It is not the Father of the New Testament story that receives the sacrifice, but the power of being inside everyone of us. The God of the Old Testament is the "God of Theism,"[117] a God of love and condescension who guides his people because he loves them. The God of Jesus, his "Father," is likewise the God of a religion, to whom we have a relationship of reverence, adoration and even of friendship, but this is not the God of the Cross as depicted by Tillich. The symbol of the Cross reaches above the God of theism. For "the Crucified . . . cried to God who remained his God after the God of confidence had left him in the darkness of doubt and meaninglessness."[118] Taking its cue from this, the "Church under the Cross," as now interpreted, "raises itself in its message and its devotion to the God above the God of theism without sacrificing its concrete symbols."[119] The Church "stands for the power of being-itself or for the God who transcends the

115. *The Religious Situation*, p. 213.   116. Art. 24, n. 25.
117. *The Courage to Be*, p. 188.   118. *Ibid.*
119. *Ibid.*

God of all religions."[120] In this view, the God of theism, the God who has been adored in all religions and who, as it was hitherto believed by Christians, revealed himself in Jesus the Christ, is only a convenient source of concrete symbols for a philosophical theory concerning the "power to be." It itself is a symbol of the power to be, the fathomless abyss and ground of being on the surface of which our consciousness floats. Pascal thought that the Living God is not the God of the philosophers, but the God of Abraham, Isaac and Jacob. Pascal could not be more mistaken, so are we told: "*Against* Pascal I say: The God of Abraham, Isaac and Jacob and the God of the philosophers is the same God."[121] In perfect consistency Tillich should have said: The God of Abraham, Isaac and Jacob, the God of the prophets, the God of Jesus, the God of the Christian tradition, is a concrete but inadequate symbol for the God of the philosophers. The myth of the Cross is a convenient image for the death of the God of theism and his replacement by the power to be.

Tillich's analysis of the main Christian symbols corresponds exactly to his analysis of faith. Faith is simply a more or less confused awareness of being-itself, beneath all the concrete experiences of man's existence. The Christ represents this ground of being when it is known in an intense intuition and feeling of regeneration. The Christ is thus the New Being, the New Creation. He is also the Word of God; for the New Being is identical with being-itself, the Ultimate, for which the word "God" provides a traditional symbol. He is the Word because he represents the ground of being in its second aspect, its life-containing capacity. He is crucified because the Cross is an adequate symbol of self-transcendence through self-sacrifice, of the subservience of conscious being to being-itself. The Christ is therefore not merely the God of Christianity; he is the universal God for whom all have been seeking and whom all have obscurely perceived even in their ignorance and doubt.

How close Tillich's position is to Protestantism we may gather from John Calvin's protest: There are those who "claim that truth

120. *Ibid.*
121. *Biblical Religion and the Search for Ultimate Reality*, p. 85.

may be held in error, light in blindness and knowledge in ignorance." Of Tillich's faith in the ground of being of the philosophers above the concrete being of the Christian God we may say with Calvin: "But it is mockery to attribute the name of faith to pure ignorance."[122] Calvin was objecting to the concept of implicit faith found in Roman Catholic theology. How much more to the point his protest is as we face the even more remotely implicit faith of Paul Tillich with its ontological transcendence of concrete symbols!

122. *Institutes*, Book III, ch. 2, n. 3.

Chapter V

CHRISTOLOGY AS HISTORY

OUR analysis of the main symbols of Christianity has prescinded from the question of the historical character of the Christian faith. One could treat Christianity as a set of religious symbols with no historical content. The notion of symbol, as such, implies neither historicity nor non-historicity. The symbols may have been actually realized in the historical situations of human beings, or again they may not. The Cross could be a suggestive symbol of self-transcendence even if Jesus the Christ had not died on a cross. A historical problem is thus raised by Christology: was the Christ a historical figure whose life is historically documented?

The historical elements of Christology may also be seen from another viewpoint. Even if we avoid the question of the historical existence of Jesus, we cannot bypass the patent fact of the world-historical importance of Christology. To define the true scope of this importance is a second problem and, in Tillich's opinion, *the* Christological problem of today. It has for us the same importance as the problem of the two natures of Christ in the fifth century. "We are no more able to continue the old discussions concerning the unity of two natures or two wills in Christ, except in transforming them into the problem of our present situation, that is the problem of an interpretation of history."[1] The question of the two natures in Christ must now be posited as concerning the human and the divine in history. Insofar as the picture of the Christ dominates history, this remains a Christological problem.

Tillich points to a third meaning of the historical problem when he writes: "The Church as a living reality must permanently mediate its eternal foundation with the demands of the historical

1. *The Interpretation of History*, p. 261.

situation."[2] The doctrine of the Christ should not be announced in the abstract, as though formulas expressing it were understandable in all times and all places. The presentation of the message should, on the contrary, be partly moulded on the sort of question which arises from each historical situation. Christianity is historical in the sense that its timeless good tidings are announced in time; if the content of the message does not change, the form does according to circumstances of time and place. Thus there exists a new historical problem: the influence of history on the forms of the Christian doctrine.

The aforementioned three problems are all Christological. Yet the third would demand an extensive inquiry into the nature of theology and of dogma. We shall treat it explicitly in the next chapter. The second problem, that of the historical power of Christology, changes the usual perspective of theologians. Few include an interpretation of history in their Christological treatises. They commonly restrict the historical problem of Christ to a study of the documents of early Christianity and their reliability as historical sources. This—the first problem we have mentioned—is given due importance in Paul Tillich's theology, and we shall meet it in its proper place. Yet Tillich's emphasis is not on an empirical or scientific study of documents. Supposing the documents were discarded, the picture of Jesus as the Christ would remain in the Christian conscience and it would still be true that this picture has dominated history for twenty centuries. The second is therefore the basic historical problem.

To recognize this is one thing; to deem it as important for our times as the question of the two natures of Christ in the patristic era is another. Fortunately Tillich explains his point very clearly in two important studies, *The Interpretation of History* and *The Religious Situation*. The universal quest for the Christ shapes the cultures of the various historical periods in different patterns. Many factors, among which fate and freedom are constantly interplaying, have influenced successive cultures. Always linked, these cultures have nevertheless evolved. Like the surface of the ocean, culture is always the same and always changing. Always

2. *The Protestant Era*, p. xiv.

the same, it formulates the quest for the Christ, the longing for the eternal, the search for the New Being. Always changing, it alters the stress, colour or intensity of this continuous seeking. In *The Religious Situation*, Tillich analyses the religious dimension of contemporary culture. "Every spiritual phenomenon of a period expresses its eternal content and one of the most important characteristics of a time has been defined when we have discovered which of the various aspects of culture is most expressive of its real meaning."[3] The main aspect of modern-day culture is that it is caught in a flux. At the end of a period of autonomy, it hesitates between a return to heteronomy and a search for theonomy. Secular culture has reached the end of its tether in the professed atheism of many modern movements. Shall culture create new forms of heteronomy as in Fascism or Communism? Shall it swim back to old forms of heteronomy as in Roman Catholicism, seen by Tillich? Or shall it go on criticizing autonomy in the name of the Protestant principle and thus discover theonomy?—which ultimately means: on what principles is modern culture going to interpret itself? How will it choose to read history? The interpretation of history lies at the core of the modern situation. Tillich, not content with this general insight, elaborates his thesis in *The Interpretation of History*. Today the interpretation of history is a philosophical, a political and a theological question, and Tillich has investigated all of these. Coming out of the German philosophical tradition, he has been influenced by the historical thinking of the German idealists. With Hegel history became a philosophical category and so it has remained, in spite of the many corrections that have modified and even replaced the Hegelian synthesis. With Marx and his followers, the philosophical categories of history invaded the realm of practical politics; our decade has seen a form of Marxism raised to world-power. In theology, the recurring question of the Church's relation to culture and the modern emphasis on eschatology correspond to this primacy of history in modern thinking. If Christology implies an inquiry into the relation of Jesus the Christ to human thought and human life, then the

3. *The Religious Situation*, p. 37.

Christological question today is essentially historical: does the message of the New Being in Jesus as the Christ convey a reading of history which would be impossible without the Christ?

It would hardly be possible to grasp the depth of Tillich's insight into history apart from the sense of time which underlies many of his writings. To speak of history is to speak of past, present and future. But nobody knows either past or future except from a point which is, for him, the present. Thus "the present is the past"; and it is equally true to say that "the present is the future."[4] The interrelationship of the past out of which the present is born, and the future of which the present is the matrix, constitutes the problem of *time*. This problem is further complicated by the fact that it is not enough to say, "The present is the past," and "the present is the future." Besides a horizontal relation to past and future, the present has a vertical relation to the eternal: "the present is eternity."[5] Time would not be important if it was deprived of an ultimate meaning, if it was "but a moving, a flowing, a becoming and decaying."[6] Thus the experience of the flow of time raises two distinct, yet connected, questions. To be on "the mysterious boundary-line of the present,"[7] between the past which is no longer and the future which is not yet, raises the question of the meaning of time. "The borderline is the truly propitious place for acquiring knowledge."[8] Placed at the border-line which is the present, man tries to find the sense of the past and the direction of the future. He attempts to determine this sense in history. History, in Tillich's perspective, is what gives meaning to time. "The movement towards something, towards the new, which is claimed as well as expected, is constitutive" of history.[9] In other words, history is essentially interpretative. It is not a collection of documents, a museum of facts, or a list of dates. This may be called erudition, but it is not history. Nor is history the past events themselves: it is their interpreted sense as we may discern it.

4. *Ibid.*, pp. 32-33.   5. *Ibid.*, p. 35.
6. *Ibid.*   7. *Ibid.*
8. *The Interpretation of History*, p. 3.   9. *Ibid.*, p. 59.

As to the dimension of eternity in the present, it is religion, properly speaking. The flow of time "is really important if it has an unconditional meaning, an unconditional depth, an unconditioned reality."[10] As we have seen, the perception of the Unconditional is the work of faith. Faith perceives the eternal dimension of the present. No interpretation of history can be ultimately satisfactory, unless it grasps the meaning of past and future in the light of the present as eternity. In this sense an interpretation of history is always implicitly religious.

It is clear, then, that the concept of history has far-reaching implications. If history is the meaning of time, it must be creative. The seasonal cycle of nature is not history, for it needs no explanation: it is "complete as being, without lack, without need for something new or something better or something perfect."[11] Instead, history deals with time as past and future seen through the present. And the future, since it is not yet, will be new. Accordingly, there is no history without the choice of a future; and there is no choice without freedom. History gives meaning to time through the mediation of a free decision or choice. "The new, which occurs wherever history occurs, is meaning. In creating meaning, being rises above itself. For meaning—as we use the word here—is realized by freedom and only by freedom; in creating meaning, being gains freedom from itself, from the necessity of its nature. History exists where meaning is realized by freedom. The new which is produced by history is really new because it is produced by freedom. Freedom is the leap in which history transgresses the realm of pure being and creates meaning."[12] History is not accounted for only in terms of development: "There are many developments in history, but insofar as they are mere developments, they are not yet history."[13] History is not made of everything that historians know about the past; it is made only of what they know as meaningful. And as there is no ultimate meaning except in relation to the eternal, history is made of what, in the development of man's free decisions, is

10. *The Religious Situation*, p. 35.
11. *The Interpretation of History*, p. 272.
12. *Ibid.*, p. 273.   13. *Ibid.*, p. 274.

revelatory of the Unconditional. In a sense therefore one must say that "only when viewed as history of salvation has history an absolute meaning."[14]

How then do we know history? Not through erudition without reflection; and not by reflection without erudition. If we wish to understand the meaning of past events, we must first be acquainted with those events. But this is only preliminary. On the other hand, once we have perceived a meaning, it "cannot be brought to the surface of historical reports."[15] If it could, the meaning of history would become one of the many incidental factors of a historical situation. It would no longer explain them in their eternal relevance. "It must remain background and depth."[16] In other words, only he who participates in a meaning can grasp or be grasped by it. Only he who is committed to the ultimate meaning of history, to the eternal, can understand history. Insofar as interpreting history involves the future, it requires "creative will." This point of view is not detached, but "directed and tense."[17] "Whoever would maintain the ideal of pure observation must content himself with numbers and names, statistics and newspaper clippings. He might collect thousands of things which could be verified, but he would not for that reason be able to understand what is happening in the present."[18] A truly historical judgment requires participation in the developing, creating and meaning-giving process: "One is enabled to speak of that which is most vital in the present, of that which makes the present a generative force, only insofar as one immerses oneself in the creative process which brings the future forth out of the past."[19] This holds true of the history of any foreign land or of any past event: "We actually know history only as we stand active within it, and as we are able to transform every foreign history into our own history through our own decisions."[20] The meaning of time which history discerns requires the creative power of experience. Where direct experience is impossible, it requires empathy, which is itself a form of experience.

14. *Ibid.*, p. 98.   15. *Ibid.*
16. *Ibid.*   17. *The Religious Situation*, p. 34.
18. *Ibid.*   19. *Ibid.*   20. *The Interpretation of History*, p. 281.

Paul Tillich's conception of history as meaningful time, or, what amounts to the same, as the perception of the depth of events, is essentially religious. He seeks for an "absolute judgment"[21] of the "absolute meaning"[22] of time, for the eternal and, so to say, eschatological dimension of past, present and future. Hence Tillich is to be distinguished, not only from those who see history as erudition about the past, but also from those who separate the flow of time and its eternal depth. In his own words, he is neither a naturalist nor a supra-naturalist. Naturalism, in this context, makes history a mere matter of facts, without transcendent meaning. Supra-naturalism adds religion, faith, revelation to history as something from above which is involved in the flow of time without truly redeeming it; the Church is viewed as a hieratic structure above time; faith is a God-given datum above the free and creative choice of man; history and salvation are juxtaposed. In Tillich's eyes, history is always the history of salvation; nature as such is self-transcending; the meaning of events is that these events reveal a vista on the eternal, without ceasing to be the very stuff of this world.

Though history discloses the revelatory dimension of events, not all events are equally revelatory. Not all are caught in a revelatory constellation. Not all have inspired the ecstasy of faith. Paul Tillich's conception of history must therefore be completed by another of the typical elements of his thinking. A recurrent theme in his works has puzzled many of his readers. Not the least reason for this is that Tillich who, as he tells us in an autobiographical essay, experienced at one time "enthusiasm for the Greek language,"[22a] has given it a Greek name. A number of his essays deal with the notion of *kairos*—a key to his Christological understanding of history.

The Greeks distinguished between *chronos* and *kairos*. Both terms refer to time, but with different connotations. As Tillich explains it, *chronos* is simply the flow of time. It is *kairos* which is meaningful. Let us remember that we are seeking for the Ulti-

---

21. *Ibid.*, p. 170.   22. *Ibid.*, p. 279.
22a. *Ibid.*, p. 17.

mate that must pierce through time, that must be pointed at by historical events. We are in search of an unconditioned meaning of time. And "to speak of an unconditioned meaning is to speak of that which transcends the process of mere becoming . . . it is to speak of that which supports the times but is not subject to them."[23] The Unconditioned is only perceived through a free decision. Ecstasy is liberating because man's fate is freely engaged in it. There is no perception or reception of the Ultimate unless the total personality is freely committed to it. The term *kairos*, as used by Tillich, designates the appeal of a historical event to man's free decision. When there is an element of miracle in a given situation, in response to which the mind will ecstatically reach the meaning of this moment of time, time is no longer merely *chronos*, it is *kairos*. "Time is all-decisive, not empty time, pure expiration; not the mere duration either, but rather qualitatively fulfilled time, the moment that is creation and fate. We call this fulfilled moment, the moment of time approaching us as fate and decision, *kairos*."[24] "A moment of time, an event, deserves the name of *kairos*, fullness of time in the precise sense, if it can be regarded in its relation to the Unconditioned, if it speaks of the Unconditioned, and if to speak of it is at the same time to speak of the Unconditioned. To look at a time thus is to look at it in its truth."[25] It is conceivable that each moment of time ultimately possesses this ·dimension. Yet not each has inspired an unconditional acceptance of its eternal dimension. Just as a man's life goes through a number of revelatory situations separated by periods of varying length, so does the life of mankind. *Kairos* reveals the religious dimension of an era. One should not consider it as arbitrary. Man does not create the meaning of an era. He only perceives it, even though he does so as a result of his own commitment to that era and of his involvement in it. Tillich wants to avoid superficial interpretations. Historians should not see a period only in terms of its military victories and defeats. They should plunge into its depth. *Kairos* is "the fate of the time, the point at which time is disturbed by eternity."[26] The know-

23. *The Religious Situation*, p. 7. 24. *The Interpretation of History*, p. 129.
25. *Ibid.*, p. 173. 26. *Ibid.*, p. 174.

ledge which is born of it has not grown "out of accidental arbitrary events of a period but out of the period's basic significance."[27] *Kairos* is not a historical theory concerning the influence of a politician's decisions at a given time. *Kairos* exists only because "the eternal is taken up into the forms of time, it becomes an existential form, temporal and contemporary. The Other, that in which every time transcends itself, becomes an individual event, a present in time. That which is not time becomes time, that which is not an existential form becomes an existing form."[28] *Kairos* is a moment of time pierced by the eternal. Then the eternal is perceived through temporal events, the Unconditional is discerned under the conditions of existence. Paul Tillich believes that the post-World War I period was such a time; and in numerous passages he insists that it has been the tragedy of our period that the breakthrough of the eternal was then better understood by the secular socialist movement than by the Churches.[29] At this point those who trust the Churches more than socialism may have doubts about his conception of *kairos*. For how do we know that *kairos* is *kairos*? How are we sure of the message of a time? How can we ascertain the ultimate meaning of a given historical event or era?

The answer is of course that the question is unanswerable. We cannot say "how" any more than we can give a proof, acceptable in a court of law, that we have experienced the ecstasy of faith. And yet, we always know when we know the Unconditional. The certainty, though uncommunicable, is nevertheless certain. Tillich expresses this in a very telling way. After asking if the message of *kairos* can be an error, he continues: "The message is always an error; for it sees something immediately imminent which, considered in its ideal aspect, will never become a reality and which, considered in its real aspect, will be fulfilled only in long periods of time. And yet the message of the *kairos* is never an error; for where the *kairos* is proclaimed as a prophetic message, it is already present; it is impossible for it to be proclaimed in power without its having grasped those who proclaim it."[30]

27. *Ibid.*
29. *The Protestant Era*, p. 49.
28. *The Religious Situation*, pp. 38-39.
30. *Ibid.*, p. 51.

Since *kairos* reveals the meaning of a period by showing the form then taken by the message of the eternal, the question may be asked if there is a *kairos* powerful enough to reveal the meaning of the whole of history, embracing past, present and future. Can we find such a *kairos* as will reveal the universal scope of time? In Greek terms, what is the relation between *kairos*, the eternal dimension of a given period, and *logos*, the timeless meaning of being?

A preliminary answer may be given. The concept of a centre of history is common to many cultures. And the centre of history is precisely conceived as the identity of a given *kairos* with the universal *logos*. "The centre of history is the place where the meaning-giving principle of history is seen."[31] The notion of a centre of history is found in cultures that have sought the New Being in the weft and woof of the historical process itself. "Thus the centre of history for the Jews is the exodus from Egypt and its main event, the treaty with God on Mount Sinai; for the Persians, the appearance of Zarathustra; and for the Moslems, Mohammed's flight from Mecca to Medina."[32] All these are Western types of cultures. On the other hand, Eastern cultures, like Brahmanism and Buddhism, have sought for the New Being above, rather than within, history. For them there is no centre of history; and there is no history either, for time is then meaningless and history is the meaning of time.[33] It is significant that cultures that have denied a meaning to time have also left undeveloped the notion of history and that of its centre. Historical cultures have been open to the notion of a centre of history in which the Unconditional would be perceived within existence, the eternal within time. If there is history, there is "a point in which history reveals its meaning."[34] Were there no such point, there would be no history. Time would be empty, meaningless. And this point, when it has been found, is the centre of history. "When God himself appears in a moment of time, when he himself subjects

31. *The Interpretation of History*, p. 250.
32. *Ibid.*, p. 258.
33. *Systematic Theology* II, pp. 87–88.
34. *The Interpretation of History*, p. 249.

himself to the flux of time, the flux of time is conquered. And if this happens in *one* moment of time, then *all* moments of time receive another significance."[35]

If history is seen as time between a beginning and an end, "we can say that not beginning and end determine the centre, as is the case in spatial measurements, but that the centre of history determines its beginning and end from the meaning of an historical process."[36] This means that history lasts as long as the revelatory power of its centre is experienced, first by anticipation, then by participation. Before this there may be a pre-history, a meaningless time or, rather, a time whose meaning was unperceived After it, one could conceive of a post-history, another stretch of time deprived of a centre and which itself perhaps would be a pre-history before another centre is expected. All this, however, is mere speculation; "such a possibility is purely abstract."[37] It helps us to see, nevertheless, that the important point of history is that which gives it meaning, its centre. Everything else revolves around it. Properly speaking, the centre of history is constitutive of it: the meaning of a period arises out of a revelatory situation. "History is constituted by the fact that its centre is constituted, or—since this is not an arbitrary act—by the fact that a centre proves to be a centre through creating history."[38]

By a series of well-timed steps, Paul Tillich has led us to the brink of the Christological affirmation. First he has defined history as the meaning of time. Second, he has shown that this meaning comes to light in moments of intense experience of which one may say, "This is the acceptable time, the *kairos*." At that precise moment, the eternal invades the temporal. Third, he has shown that while each period of history may receive its meaning from such a *kairos*, the whole span of history can receive it only from a universal *kairos* which will be its centre. The fourth step, to which we are now coming, is that Jesus as the Christ is the centre of history, "the point where salvation manifests itself as the content of history."[39]

35. *The New Being*, p. 167.   36. *The Interpretation of History*, p. 250.
37. *Ibid.*, p. 251.   38. *Ibid.*, p. 250.   39. *Ibid.*, p. 256.

Before explaining this, I should mention an intriguing point in *The Interpretation of History*. Paul Tillich shows that the centre of history cannot be conceived of as future: "It cannot be sought for in the future, for the meaning of the future is determined by it."[40] We think that the future will be meaningful only on the basis of a principle which we already possess. But this is not all: "The centre cannot lie in the present either."[41] For the present has no historical meaning unless it explains the past too. It has such a meaning "only if it is the point in which are joined the historical fate which is born in the past, and the historical decision which provides the future."[42] This is to say that the present must itself refer to some meaningful point in the past, to a past *kairos* in the light of which the present is meaningful. "No present can be a historical centre for itself."[43] As a matter of fact, every centre of history in any religion or culture has always been seen as a point of reference in the past. If we remember that in Tillich's analysis of time, the present is, in a sense, both the past and the future, this remark on the past character of the centre of history is not as striking as it may seem. At any moment when we are grasped by the power of *kairos*, we are in contact with a "super-historical reality," and experience "the presence of the past in the present."[44] The conclusion which this imposes on Christology does not affect our consciousness of the centre of history in Jesus as the Christ. But it does affect Tillich's view of the self-consciousness of the Christ. For if the advent of the Christ in Jesus is the centre of history for us, it cannot have been the centre of history for Jesus. The implications of this will claim our attention later.

The Christological affirmation is that Jesus as the Christ is the centre of history. His manifestation was the *kairos* in which the meaning of the whole of history was perceived. "When Jesus says that the right hour has come, that the kingdom of God is at hand, he pronounces the victory over the law of vanity. *This hour is not subject to the circle of life and death and all the other circles of vanity.*"[45] In the life of Jesus, the hour of Calvary

40. *Ibid.*
42. *Ibid.*, p. 257.
44. *Ibid.*
41. *Ibid.*
43. *Ibid.*
45. *The New Being*, p. 167.

particularly emphasizes the breakthrough of the eternal. "The event at Golgotha is one which concerns the universe, including all nature and all history. . . . Since this moment the universe is no longer what it was; nature has received another meaning; history is transformed and you and I are no more, and should not be any more, what we were before."[46] The meaning of history has been revealed. From that time on all things are new. "When the apostles say that Jesus is the Christ, they mean that in him the new eon which cannot become old is present. Christianity lives through the faith that within it there is the new which is not just another new thing but rather the principle and representation of all really new in man and history."[47] The homiletic passages where Tillich announces this mystery are eloquent. The philosophical texts are no less telling. That history is Christology and that Christology is history forms the sum and substance of Tillich's view of history. "History is conditioned by the appearance of an unconditioned meaning not as a demand but as an existent, not as an idea but as the temporal and paradoxical anticipation of the ultimate perfection."[48] "The problem of history combines with the Christological problem. . . . Christology, being the definition and description of this (central) point in rational terms, is at the same time the basis on which the interpretation of history rests."[49] In saying this, Tillich does not claim that history may demonstrate Christology. We should always remember that a revelatory situation is not subject to the scalpel of scientific analysis. A historical record cannot classify the centre of history along with other, more peripheral, events. One can perceive the centre and discern the meaning of history only as one can receive a revelation, in ecstasy and faith.

On the one hand, Christology may show the universal dimension implied in the event of the Christ. Christianity gives "an abstract and universal meaning to the Christological idea"; this abstract meaning must be justified. So is it "if therewith the universal claim implied in the constitution of a centre of history is expressed."[50] Theologians must show that the Christological

46. *Ibid.*, pp. 176-79.   47. *The Shaking of the Foundations*, p. 186.
48. *The Interpretation of History*, p. 262.   49. *Ibid.*, p. 256.   50. *Ibid.*, p. 259.

affirmation solves the dilemma of all mankind, that it provides a satisfactory answer to all the forms that the quest for the New Being has taken. This Tillich does in his *Systematic Theology* II, where he points out that "the historical type of the expectation of the New Being embraces itself and the non-historical type, while the non-historical is unable to embrace the historical type."[51] Christology unites "the horizontal direction of the expectation of the New Being with the vertical one."[52] The horizontal, or historical, direction characterizes Western thought, while the vertical, or mystical, direction marks Eastern thought. The Christian faith affirms the Christ, not only as the historical Messiah, but also as the Man on the Clouds of the prophet Daniel; it affirms him both as Saviour and divine Wisdom. In him were the *kairos*, the dynamic advent of the eternal, and the *logos*, the universal transcosmic presence of the divine. Thanks to this, Christology does not appear "as a strange insertion within the trend of ideas concerning the philosophy of history."[53]

On the other hand, it is not a matter of proof that Jesus as the Christ is effectively the centre of history. Christology is a "possible answer to the basic question implied in history, an answer, of course, which can never be proved by arguments, but is a matter of decision and fate."[54] He who is confronted by the picture of the Christ in the Christian faith is caught up in a revelatory situation. Not only his own past, but the whole past of mankind helps to determine his answer: this is the element of fate implied in the situation. And the future is at stake, for its meaning or its meaninglessness depends on the answer: this is the element of decision. "Being grasped by the centre of history means being grasped without limitations and conditions, by an absolute power. The fate in which we are grasped by a centre of history in such a way is named 'predestination' in religious terminology; the decision in which we grasp that which grasps us, is named faith."[55] Christ is indeed the centre of history, but "only for faith."[56] Historical

51. *Systematic Theology* II, p. 89.   52. *Ibid.*
53. *The Interpretation of History*, p. 259.
53. *Ibid.*   54. *Ibid.*
55. *Ibid.*, p. 260.   56. *Ibid.*

erudition cannot reach this in any document. To know the ultimate meaning of history requires commitment, courage and decision, the decision for the Christ. To one who has not been caught in this revelation, Christology is foolishness and scandal. To one who has been, Christ is the final revelation.

We already know that the centre of history gives meaning to past, present and future; it constitutes history as the meaning of time. The scope of the Christological affirmation should be explored further.

The historical relevance of Christology may be expressed in terms of revelation. Revelation is the reception of an insight into the ground of being. These insights are many; many factors may occasion or convey them. The concept of revelation, then, in the writings of Paul Tillich, is not a necessarily Christian concept. But we are soon confronted with the exclusive claims of Christianity: "Christianity claims to be based on the revelation of Jesus as the Christ as the final revelation."[57] Tillich warns us that "final" in this context is not tantamount to "last." Revelatory situations are not exhausted by the coming of the Christ. We do not assert that there can be no ecstasy and no faith after the Christ. On the contrary, Tillich's analysis of life shows the ground of being as constantly piercing the crust of existence and making itself experienced in the depths of our being. What is true of mankind is equally true of the Church: "Christianity often has affirmed, and certainly should affirm, that there is continuous revelation in the history of the Church."[58] The whole meaning of preaching the word of God consists in announcing a revelatory message. Yet if this is true of Christian preaching, it is equally true that the mission of the whole Church must be referred back to the event of the Christ. No preaching can be revelatory unless it is grasped by the power of the Christ. No word of man becomes word of God unless the Christ takes it, so to say, in charge. The final revelation in the Christ, therefore, does not mean simply "last." Rather, it means last genuine.[59] "There can be no reve-

57. *Systematic Theology* I, p. 132.
58. *Ibid.*   59. *Ibid.*

lation in the history of the Church whose point of reference is not Jesus as the Christ."[60] Secondly, it means that we do not refer to the last genuine revelation as to a past event; we refer to it as to an event by whose power we are still grasped. Thus, the final revelation "means the decisive, fulfilling, unsurpassable revelation, that which is the criterion of all others."[61]

A necessary mark of this final revelation is its universal contemporaneity. "Revelation is revelation to me in my concrete situation, in my historical reality."[62] Christianity does not ask anyone to make an imposssible leap two thousand years back. Such a journey through historical documents may provide erudite knowledge of an obscure past event, but it can in no way reveal the power to be which was present in the Christ. To be present in Palestine when Jesus was there is impossible. And yet the Christ will not be revelatory to me unless I experience him. He is not an abstraction, but a revelatory person. He can be known only through a person-to-person relationship. Tillich reaches the conclusion that something, in the revelatory situation of Jesus as the Christ, must be permanently present and thus become contemporary to me and to all men. "He who is the Christ is contemporaneous, or he is not the Christ."[63]

We have posited, in personal terms, the question of the criterion of ultimate revelation. What must be contemporary to me in the Christ-situation is that which makes it the final revelation. Faith is not concerned with details of Christ's existence, but with its meaning. The centre of history is not central through accidental happenings, but through its essential purport. Under the conditions of existence, however, meaning is made obscure by its very medium itself. Existence is ambiguous. It is abyss and depth, negation and affirmation. The individual contradicts the universal. The concrete opposes the abstract. The message of the final revelation must be both concrete and universal; it must be set in an existential situation if it is to reach men who are caught in the snare of existence; and it must be universal, above existence, if it is to reach men outside of the small circle of the intimates of

---

60. *Ibid.*
61. *Ibid.*, p. 133.
62. *The Protestant Era*, p. 81.
63. *Ibid.*, p. 82.

Jesus of Nazareth during his earthly life. The criterion of the final revelation will therefore be given when its bearer negates himself as a limited and limiting being to affirm the eternal. "A revelation is final if it has the power of negating itself without losing itself."[64] The same thought is beautifully expressed in an important passage which epitomizes all of Tillich's doctrine on the Christ as the medium of the final revelation:

> The question of the final revelation is the question of a medium of revelation which overcomes its own finite conditions by sacrificing them, and itself with them. He who is the bearer of the final revelation must surrender his finitude—not only his life but also his finite power and knowledge and perfection. In doing so, he affirms that he is the bearer of the final revelation (the "Son of God" in classical terms). He becomes completely transparent to the mystery he reveals.[65]

This gives us one characteristic of the medium of the final revelation: self-negation. But who can negate himself so completely that only the eternal shines through him? One can give up only what one has mastered. Hence a second characteristic: the bearer of the final revelation must be perfect, that is, perfectly united to the power to be, in living communication with the ground of being, in constant communion with being-itself. "But in order to surrender himself completely, he must possess himself completely. And only he can possess—and therefore surrender—himself completely who is united with the ground of his being and meaning without separation and disruption."[66] This is precisely what we find in the Christ: complete surrender because of complete self-possession in the power of the ground of being. "In the picture of Jesus as the Christ we have the picture of a man who possesses these qualities, a man who, therefore, can be called the medium of final revelation."[67] Nowhere is the picture clearer than in the symbol of the Cross, where Jesus sacrificed himself as Jesus to himself as the Christ, himself as finite to himself as the bearer of the New Being.

64. *Systematic Theology* I, p. 133.   65. *Ibid.*
66. *Ibid.*   67. *Ibid.*

The Christological affirmation may also be expressed in terms of *kairos*. Christology claims to provide the ultimate meaning of history. Or, rather, it claims that in Jesus as the Christ the ultimate meaning of history was revealed. What is that meaning?

In Jesus as the Christ a decision was made which decided the orientation of history. Jesus the Christ, accepting his self-effacement, affirmed ultimate being. He unveiled the ultimate truth. He pronounced an ultimate judgment on which the destiny of mankind and history depends. Paul Tillich devotes some pages of *The Interpretation of History* to exploring the nature of knowledge. Among other things, he notes that the Catholic Middle Ages developed an objective, "super-rational and static"[68] conception of knowledge. In contrast, "there is no Protestant conception of knowledge."[69] This absence results from the difficulty of elaborating a conception of knowledge which is "irrational and dynamic."[70] Yet this is what knowledge is. The knowledge that is reached in the intense experience of *kairos*, the knowledge that reveals the basic meaning of a historical period, is relative to a decision, namely to the "yes" which accepts the meaning of *kairos*. If the event of Jesus as the Christ is truly the universal *kairos*, the acceptable time in which the meaning of all history is achieved by the self-transcendence of the Christ, then the knowledge which derives from it must have a universal character. It must be a "knowledge of knowledge,"[71] to which every other knowledge must be referred, the criterion of every judgment.

In Tillich's intellectual universe there precisely is a judgment that underlies all others. It is "the expression of the relation of knowledge to the Unconditional."[72] "The judgment that is removed from ambiguity, the judgment of absolute unequivocal truth, can be only the fundamental judgment about the relationship of the Unconditioned and the conditioned."[73] This "absolute standpoint,"[74] or absolute judgment, is the content of the message of the Christ; it judges every other judgment and is the criterion

68. *The Interpretation of History*, p. 135.
69. *Ibid.*
70. *Ibid.*
71. *Ibid.*, p. 170.
72. *Ibid.*
73. *Ibid.*
74. *Ibid.*, p. 171.

of every other knowledge. "The content of this judgment is just this—that our subjective thinking never can reach the unconditioned truth, that it must always remain in the realm of ambiguity. This judgment is plainly the absolute judgment which is independent of all its forms of expression, even of the one by which it is expressed here. It is the judgment which constitutes truth as truth."[75] In these somewhat abstract terms, Tillich does nothing but express the meaning which is symbolically contained in the Cross and historically realized on Golgotha: the human condition never is the Unconditional; only self-negation, the knowledge of one's ambiguities, does justice to the Ultimate. Jesus is the Christ only because he transcends himself. The Unconditional appears under the conditions of existence only by pointing out the vanity of existence. The supreme *kairos* was precisely a moment of time when this absolute judgment on man was pronounced. "The *kairos*, the fateful moment of knowledge, is absolute insofar as it places one at this moment before the absolute decision for or against the truth."[76]

The centre of history in the Christ as the final revelation, and the centre of history as the standard of all knowledge both converge on one point: the Cross. "The decisive manifestation of the divine . . . [can be] but a protest against the claim of every finite form to be absolute, i.e., the Word of the Cross."[77] The Cross, in this context, is a symbol. It also is a fact. Reminiscing on the beginnings of his theological effort Tillich remarks: "My Christology and my Dogmatics were determined by the interpretation of the Cross of Christ as the event of history in which this divine judgment over the world became concrete and manifest."[78] His sermons often echo this certainty of the presence of the eternal in time through the Christ. "Only a new reality can make us whole, breaking into the old one, reconciling it with itself. It is the humanly incredible, ecstatic, often defeated, but never conquered faith of Christianity, that this new reality which was always at work in history has appeared in fullness

75. *Ibid.*, p. 170.   76. *Ibid.*, p. 175.
77. *Ibid.*, p. 234.   78. *Ibid.*, p. 32.

and power in Jesus, the Christ, the Healer and Saviour."[79] "The Christ had to suffer and die, because whenever the Divine appears in all its depths, it cannot be endured by men. . . . Even the greatest in power and wisdom could not more fully reveal the Heart of God and the heart of man than the Crucified has done already. Those things have been revealed once for all. 'It is finished.' In the face of the Crucified all the 'more' and all the 'less,' all progress and all approximation, are meaningless. Therefore we can say of him alone: he is the new reality; he is the end; he is the Messiah. To the Crucified alone we can say, 'Thou art the Christ.' "[80]

Pushing the analysis further, let us now ask, What exactly is this message of the Cross which gives meaning to history? Paul Tillich has expressed it in terms of an ultimate revelation, in terms of the ultimate *kairos*, in terms of absolute knowledge. The Cross has shown it as the self-transcendence of the Christ, which he affirmed in "the waste of an uncalculated self-surrender,"[81] in "the most complete and the most holy waste."[82] In all this we may recognize an old friend. The themes which have just been brought up have already been heard. They formed the common thread of our preceding chapters. In a word, the meaning of history, as manifested in the Cross of the Christ, is the Protestant principle.

In the Cross we find a resolution of the tension between the conditioned and the Unconditional: the one shines through the other. If "every religious word is an interpretation of the tension between the conditionally and the unconditionally real, between realism and self-transcendence,"[83] the word from the Cross is "self-transcendent realism." As depicted in *Systematic Theology* II, the Christ exhibits no mark of "estrangement between himself and God,"[84] because he conquers estrangement; yet he displays the "marks of finitude"[85] and he participates in "the tragic element of existence."[86] In spite of this, his "permanent unity with

79. *The New Being*, p. 41.
80. *The Shaking of the Foundations*, p. 148.
81. *The New Being*, p. 47. 82. *Ibid.*, p. 49.
83. *The Protestant Era*, p. 79. 84. *Systematic Theology* II, p. 125.
85. *Ibid.*, p. 131. 86. *Ibid.*, p. 132.

God"[87] is evident. "Into this unity he accepts the negativities of existence without removing them. This is done by transcending them in the power of this unity. This is the New Being as it appears in the biblical picture of Jesus as the Christ."[88] The Protestant principle teaches that negativities must be accepted because they are already transcended in the power of God. It asserts that no created channel can convey the meaning of being-itself; yet precisely because it cannot and insofar as it cannot, it does. Being-itself is affirmed in the self-negation of created being. There is no other way of speaking of the ground of being than in the breakdown of our self-satisfied existence.

What the Protestant principle says in the realm of ontology, it repeats in the realm of knowledge: no judgment is removed from ambiguity, except the judgment that all judgment is equivocal. All "judging, questioning, answering"[89] indirectly posits an absolute judgment concerning the Unconditional: the Unconditional is, and is true, "in spite of" man's conditioned attempt to reach it. Thus "the absolute standpoint is a position which can never be taken."[90] If it were ever taken by a man, it would be conditioned by that man's estranged existence. Only the One who is unestranged from the power of being takes it: Jesus the Christ self-transcending himself on the Cross.

The Protestant principle also says—and this is another form of the negation of the finite—that every institution and event has demonic possibilities. That is, its power and meaning may be distorted from the ground of power and meaning. Yet "the Christian confession contains the certainty that the demonic has been overcome."[91] The overcoming of the demonic is another form of the Protestant principle: not even the bent and the distorted place ultimate hurdles in the path of grace. In contrast to the day-by-day experience of demonic domination, of estrangement, the Protestant principle affirms what has been experienced in the revelatory event of the Cross: "There is only one certainty, that the demonic is overcome in eternity, that in eternity the

87. *Ibid.*, p. 134.   88. *Ibid.*, p. 135.
89. *The Interpretation of History*, p. 171.
90. *Ibid.*   91. *Ibid.*, p. 107.

demonic is depth of the divine and in unity with divine clarity."[92]

The ultimate meaning of history, as manifested in the Cross of the Christ and formulated in the Protestant principle, is therefore to accept estrangement as a contrasted participation in the divine unity: "to say 'yes' to one's own life and life in general, in spite of the driving forces of fate, in spite of the insecurities of daily existence, in spite of the catastrophes of existence and the breakdown of meaning."[93] Hopes may disappoint, dreams may fade away, what we thought ours may be taken from us, life may be threatened, what we had planned may fail; yet through our choices and decisions, whether right or wrong, through our doctrines and beliefs, whether true or false, there runs a unifying thread: Protestantism points to "him who *is* the truth that liberates . . . to the being of him whose being is the truth."[94] Once again, we reach the principle of "justification by faith," to which Paul Tillich has given cosmic significance. We reach the meaning of the Cross, which stands at the heart of history.

The meaning of history, as explained by Tillich, seems rather disappointing. The sense of "let-down" recurs. If the meaning of history is that we must accept what we cannot avoid, there was really no need of the extraordinary situation of the Cross to let us know it. There was no need for Jesus the Christ to die in a supreme testimony to his unity with being-itself, if the result is only that we shall continue to do, with more awareness, what we have always done anyway. Yet this is what the matter comes to in Tillich's universe. We are in the truth even when we are not; we are in grace even when we are in sin; we are accepted even when we are estranged. This is Tillich's Protestant principle. It is, for him, the meaning of the Cross and of the entire history of man illuminated by the word from the Cross. No doubt that it is a valuable insight. But is it worth all that has prepared it? Above all, is it worth the self-sacrifice of Jesus?

Surely not. For, as Tillich himself admits, all religions have reached approximations, in practice and in theory, of the Pro-

92. *Ibid.,* p. 122.   93. *The New Being,* p. 53.
94. *Ibid.,* p. 71.

testant principle. Thus he explains that two lines, vertical and horizontal, symbolize "the meaning of human existence."[95] The vertical line points to the eternal meaning of existence, and the horizontal to its realization in history. We recognize here the Protestant principle that the eternal informs the temporal. Is this unique in Protestantism, or even in Christianity? Far from it: "Every religion necessarily has both directions, although different religions emphasize the one or the other."[96] Every religion, in other words, embodies the Protestant principle to some extent. Had there been no "final revelation," no ultimate centre of history, our world would have continued, cultures would have developed, without explicit reference to the Cross; yet they would have been unified around smaller revelations, as has been the case with non-Christian religions. The *Logos* would still have become flesh in a series of revelatory *kairoi*. "Basis and abyss" would still have been joined together; and "in the duality of both" the Unconditioned would have manifested itself.[97] The profane would still be inseparably conjoined to the holy.[98] And the tension between the two would have settled down along the lines that Tillich assigns to Church and society: "The Church is the perpetual guilty conscience of society and society is the perpetual guilty conscience of the Church."[99] Granted, the New Being would not have appeared in time; the Unconditional would not have lived under the conditions of existence. But mankind could not have missed it because, in any case, this paradox was not to be expected.

This description of what would have happened to Tillich's universe without the Christ's appearance may seem like a caricature. Actually it is the reverse of the coin we have received from Tillich. If the meaning of history is only the "justification of the unjust" extended to the moral, the intellectual and the metaphysical fields, we could, frankly, have managed without the Messiah. We could have discovered it by analysing the ground of being, by asking philosophers about being-itself. The imagina-

---

95. *The Protestant Era*, p. 186.   96. *Ibid.*
97. *The Interpretation of History*, p. 224.
98. *Ibid.*, pp. 225-26.   99. *Ibid.*, p. 227.

tive element needed for "the doctrine of the Absolute as both ground and abyss of dynamic truth"—which is the Protestant principle, the meaning of history—could have been furnished us, as Tillich reveals that it was furnished him, simply by meditating by the sea-side.[100]

Tillich is truly great in his outline of the concept of history. Bringing history to the point where it borders on the revelation is the achievement of a man of no puny vision. It is the *meaning* he assigns to history that leaves us still hungry and thirsty: we thought that we were being prepared for more.

Tillich has not exhausted the topic of Christianity as history when he has found the meaning of history in the Cross of Jesus. There remains a historical problem which is secondary in the Tillichian context. Yet I would not be surprised if theologians, Catholic as well as Protestant, have been growing increasingly nervous as the tale of this chapter was being told. For in contrast to Tillich most theologians see the basic historical problem of Christology as that of the historicity of Jesus. Is the New Testament a reliable document? Does it really establish the fact that Jesus lived, and does it truly record his sayings? Theology must give due attention to such questions. Theologians must use the scientific methods of historical criticism in order better to understand the historical purport of the Scriptures. Science cannot contradict faith; it can show that faith is not absurd, that what is believed is corroborated by documents.

Paul Tillich rejects this as the basic historical problem of Christology, and here we willingly part company with most theologians and side with him. The important problem is not to investigate the sources of Christian faith scientifically. It is to determine the relation of Christ to human history. This is more than ever true in our century. Tillich rightly emphasizes the necessity of positing the Christological question in historical terms. As it has been mentioned, he even thinks that this historical stress should displace the dogmatic question of the two natures of Christ. This can be challenged; yet, without replacing one

100. *Ibid.*, p. 8.

problem by another, we may well agree that the historical relevance of the Christological affirmation drives home more
effectively than any other today.

When this has been granted, other problems remain to be
considered. At this point we must abandon Paul Tillich to what
he calls his "radical" position. In the autobiographical essay of
The Interpretation of History, Tillich recalls that in 1911, at the age
of twenty-five, he presented some theses "to a group of theological
friends, in which I raised and attempted to answer the question,
how the Christian doctrine might be understood, if the non-
existence of the historical Jesus should become historically
probable."[101] One might view this theological escapade into the
impossible as a pardonable youthful adventure—radical, but
not to be taken too seriously. Yet, such was not the case, for in
1936 Tillich wrote: "Even today, I maintain the radicalism of this
question."[102] He also expressed a general scepticism towards the
historical study of Jesus. As to "historical inquiry into the facts
behind the rise of the biblical picture of Christ," he rapidly
dismissed it: "The exposition of those facts can only lend probability."[103] In this, Tillich was influenced by Albert Schweitzer's
somewhat negative work, *The Quest for the Historical Jesus*, an
influence that he has always acknowledged. In *Systematic Theology*
Tillich repeats his doubts concerning our historical knowledge of
Jesus. In the exhaustive historical investigations of the last century,
"the historical Jesus not only did not appear, but receded farther
and farther with every new step."[104] Schweitzer's conclusion on
this point "is still valid."[105] None of the innumerable sketches
of a historical Jesus "can claim to be a profitable picture." The
"attempt of historical criticism to find the empirical truth about
Jesus of Nazareth was a failure."[106]

This attitude towards historical investigation is more complex
than appears at face-value, and it should be neither endorsed nor
dismissed rapidly. One should distinguish several elements.

(1) We must admit with Tillich that the positive knowledge of

101. *Ibid.*, p. 33.
102. *Ibid.*, p. 34.
103. *Ibid.*, p. 265.
104. *Systematic Theology* II, p. 102.
105. *Ibid.*
106. *Ibid.*

Jesus given by history is only probable knowledge. This is not because documents are unavailable or deficient, but simply because historical study as such never gives more than a probable knowledge. Catholic theologians commonly call such knowledge a "moral certainty." Terms and words are not especially important. Whether we speak, in this case, of probability or of moral certainty, we imply that historical truth has characteristics of its own, distinguishing it from the truth of mathematics, of physics or, in another domain, of metaphysics. Historical truth is never more than a probability. If we call it a certainty, we must qualify it as "moral." To say this is to recognize the element of validity in Tillich's position here. It does not imply sharing his scepticism with regard to the historical datum concerning Christ. For Tillich the probability is "very faint," which, to my mind, does not take our knowledge of the life and times of Jesus seriously enough. In the present state of historical studies there is not the ghost of a chance that "the non-existence" of Jesus should become historically probable.

(2) Paul Tillich rightly challenges the attitude of liberal Protestantism towards history. The liberal theologians attempted to base Christianity on historical research. Tillich condemns the "road of liberal theology," along which Christ was drawn "into the realm of universal or highest humanity."[107] He became the highest expression of mankind's possibilities, "a wave (the largest perhaps) in the stream of time, subjected to its arbitrariness and ambiguity."[108] This was bound to happen once biblical critical exegesis was erected into the norm of Christian faith. Christ was no longer the centre of history, no longer the Christ. He was "the historical Jesus," or whatever vague knowledge we had of him. Tillich's stand is unimpeachable when he objects to this as a matter of principle: "The foundation of Christian belief is not the historical Jesus, but the biblical picture of the Christ. The criterion of human thought and action is not the constantly changing and artificial product of historical research, but the picture of Christ as it is rooted in ecclesiastical belief and human experience."[109]

107. *The Interpretation of History*, p. 261.
108. *Ibid.*   109. *Ibid.*, p. 34.

His opposition to "liberal dogmatics, which replaces the crucified Christ by the historical Jesus,"[110] is the only sound attitude. Christology must be the norm of history. Instead, liberal Protestantism made historical tools the norm of Christology.

(3) Tillich continues his drive on liberal Protestantism in a more questionable manner. It is perfectly true to say that the historical records of Jesus are themselves the products of faith; it is something else to conclude that they are not historically reliable, an assertion which forms the gist of the sections of *Systematic Theology* II on "the research for the historical Jesus and its failure,"[111] and on "faith and historical scepticism."[112] There is actually no logical link between the two propositions. To admit a logical link would be to admit that faith distorts facts. But faith never distorts; it interprets. This is quite different. What was wrong with the liberal theologians who were seeking for the historical Jesus was not their interest in history (though they often fell into historicism), but that their search was not guided by the religious picture of the Christ which was that of the early Church. They became bad historians, excessively negative in their conclusions, because they had first been bad theologians.

(4) It is easy to see why Tillich links the aforementioned propositions. The implied contrast between the evanescent historical Jesus and the Christ of faith corresponds too well to his own theological distinction between "Jesus as Jesus" and "Jesus as the Christ." It is not the man from Nazareth that matters, but his witness to the New Being in himself. He is the Christ insofar as he testifies to the New Being. Outside of that, he has no place in theology. Christology is not Jesusology. It is not interested in whatever happened to the man Jesus. It is interested in the fact that the disciples perceived the Christ in him. Tillich insists that "*Jesus Christ* means *Jesus who is said to be the Christ*."[113] In his self-consciousness, Jesus may not always have known that he was the Christ. On the Cross at least he despaired.[114] Looking at history in the light of this distinction between Jesus and the

---

110. *Ibid.*, p. 32.   111. *Systematic Theology* II, pp. 113-17.
112. *Ibid.*, pp. 101-107.   113. *The Shaking of the Foundations*, p. 145.
114. *Systematic Theology* II, p. 126.

Christ in him, between a man and the New Being which manifested itself through him, Tillich even imagines that maybe Jesus
was not the Christ. There was a Christ: this is a matter of revelatory experience. The Apostles experienced it directly, and we
still experience it, though indirectly. We are caught in the power
of their revelatory ecstasy, and so we cannot deny that there was,
that there is, a Christ. But the identity of the Christ and of
Jesus is not a matter of faith. It is a point of history; and it is very
questionable. "Participation, not historical argument, guarantees
the reality of the event on which Christianity is based. It guarantees a personal life in which the New Being has conquered the old
being. But it does not guarantee his name to be Jesus of
Nazareth."[115]

On this point Tillich strikes out on his own. He does not drift
along with liberal Protestantism. If his final position seems
similar to liberal Protestantism, at least the motivation is quite
different. His strictures on liberal Protestantism bear on the fallacy
that history can guarantee faith. By a strange reversal of position,
he argues that faith does not guarantee history. But this is not
because he misreads the nature of historical inquiry. It is a result
of the peculiar content of his Christology. If the New Being in
the Christ is simply a form of the Protestant principle, it does not
absolutely need a human bearer. Jesus is not necessary to the
Christ. Yet this runs contrary to the meaning of Christianity. Of
course, the Catholic faith does guarantee the identity of Jesus and
the Christ, as did the Protestant faith before liberal Protestantism.
One should carefully distinguish those historical elements that
are essential to the meaning of the Christ from those that are not;
only the former are guaranteed by faith. It represents a strange
blindness towards the historical groundwork of Christianity to
say that the identity of Jesus and the Christ is not part of the
kerygma. It is not enough to state that the original fact is the
Apostles' interpretation of Jesus. For how can we accept an
interpretation if we do not know what is to be interpreted? How
can we share the Apostles' interpretation if we choose to doubt
the identity of whom and what they interpreted?

115. p. 114.

(5) Tillich has always been concerned with what is now, since Bultmann popularized the term, called demythologization.[116] As Tillich understands it, to demythologize is not a negative process by which the truth of a myth is negated. Let us remember that a myth is, for him, a system of symbols, and that symbols derive their truth from the fact that they share the power and meaning of what they point to. In this sense, mythical does not mean untrue; it means "symbolical of the eternal."[117] To demythologize, therefore, is not to debunk a myth, but to grasp its relation to the eternal. On the one hand, literalism distorts myths by viewing them in their material elements and not in their transcendent meaning. On the other, philosophy may distort religion by suppressing myths: "The myth, if interpreted as the symbolic expression of ultimate concern, is the fundamental creation of every religious community. It cannot be replaced by philosophy."[118] In the picture of Jesus contained in the New Testament, one should distinguish faith (the faith that the Christ has appeared), myth (symbolic creations of the religious concern of the first Christians, whereby they expressed their faith in imaginative form), and history (if at least we can separate probable historical facts from mythical creations). Thus there are two successive steps in demythologizing: first, separation, if possible, of myth from the substance of faith and from facts; second, interpretation of the symbolic purport of the myth. When this is done, the myth is, in Tillich's idiom, "broken."[119] This is the only way to deal intelligently with a myth. Without abandoning or denying the myth, this method seeks to understand its meaning.

In this perspective, Christianity has all the characteristics of a myth couched in historical language: "If the Christ—a transcendent, divine being—appears in the fullness of time, lives,

116. I have touched on Tillich and Bultmann in their relation to existential philosophy in "Christianity and the Philosophies of Existence" (*Theological Studies*, March, 1954, pp. 1-16, esp. pp. 10-13). On Bultmann, cf. Myles M. Bourke: "Rudolf Bultmann's Demythologizing of the New Testament" (*Catholic Theological Society of America, Proceedings of the 10th Annual Convention*, 1957, pp. 103-31), and the bibliography therein listed.
117. *The Religious Situation*, p. 68.
118. *Dynamics of Faith*, p. 121.   119. *Ibid.*, pp. 52-53.

dies and is resurrected, this is an historical myth. . . . Christianity speaks the mythological language like every other religion. It is a broken myth, but it is a myth; otherwise Christianity would not be an expression of ultimate concern."[120] The task of theology is always to proceed to a "radical criticism of the myth."[121] For there is a recurring tendency to unbreak the myth and to read it literally again.

Tillich's scepticism concerning our historical knowledge of Jesus must be seen against this background. He is afraid lest the attempts of historians to reconstruct the historical Jesus should actually replace the meaningful myths of Christian tradition with flimsy constructions, which would themselves, eventually, acquire symbolic status, if only through their association with the name "Jesus." The new myths would not be a true Christology but a devalued Jesusology. They would not point to the New Being in the Christ, simply because symbols and myths of the New Being must grow out of a revelatory experience and cannot be invented in a laboratory. Demythologization is a necessary theological process. In particular, it protects faith against historians.

Demythologization, however, cannot be taken seriously unless it takes historians seriously. It leaves all necessary elbow-room to the higher critics. If these establish that a certain biblical report is untrue to facts, this report may still be treated as a symbol but should no longer be asserted as a fact. As we know, Tillich is chary of asserting anything concerning Jesus as a fact. Yet he maintains the religious value of the New Testament as a historical myth. The negative conclusions of historians cannot harm the symbolic meaning of a myth.

My only criticism bears on the last point. According to Tillich, Christianity is mythical. Yet should it follow that we must despair of knowing Jesus historically, or that the history of Jesus, because of its mythical depth, must be written off? Tillich is right in being sceptical of the historians' efforts to re-write the story of Jesus— but for the wrong reason. Historians cannot re-write the story because it is already written: the historical value of the New Testament is plain enough. Historians have not been able to make

120. *Ibid.*, p. 54.   121. *Ibid.*, p. 51.

its reliability improbable. Tillich has simply not been radical enough in criticizing liberal theology. He has not seen that the historians who doubt the value of the records have failed to establish their point. Here, Paul Tillich remains a child of his generation, a victim of the historicism of the last century.

This note on demythologization and its limits concludes our chapter on Christology as history. We have insisted on the properly Tillichian point of view. Only then have we paid our respects to the more usual concern about the historicity of Christ. In my view, Tillich's emphasis is right, but I have not been able to follow him in all his opinions. Yet Tillich has been thoroughly consistent. Where, as I believe, he has failed to show the meaning of history is precisely where he has been most Tillichian: his interpretation of the Christ as the appearance of essence in the conditions of existence, of the New Being in the garb of the old, has given his historical analysis a philosophical slant which is both disappointing and misleading.

A last remark. Whereas Tillich's pre-war writings highlighted the theme of *kairos*, his writings since then have been focused on the New Being. This is not a contradiction, but a significant evolution. It is as though the *kairos* which Tillich discerned in the post-World War I period had ended with World War II. Tillich, we remember, was active in Germany in the movement of "religious socialism" which, as he thought, interpreted the meaning of the time better than anything else. His exile in the United States confronted him with a very different social situation. Though still concerned about the *kairos* (the publication of *The Protestant Era* in 1948, featuring articles written between 1922 and 1945, gloriously crowned his insistence on *kairos* and the meaning of history), he now, and especially in his *Systematic Theology*, laid stress on the trans-historical New Being, insisting on the ontological more than on the historical dimension of Jesus as the Christ. This may mean that, for Tillich, the *kairos* of our period has not yet appeared. Where does history lead us? It leads us to the New Being; but through what apotheoses or catastrophes we do not know. Our age has not yet unfolded its secret message.

Chapter VI

CHRISTOLOGY AS DOGMA

AT various points of the preceding chapters we have alluded to the fate of some traditional Christian dogmas in Tillich's analysis of faith. It is significant that whereas Karl Barth calls his many-volumed synthesis a "Dogmatic," Tillich calls his a "Systematic Theology." If dogmas are at the centre of Barth's thought, they are only at the periphery of Tillich's. His main concern is, precisely, to build a "system," that is, to work out the implications of his central perception of the Protestant principle along the main lines of theological thought. Yet even though he is primarily concerned with the symbols of faith and their transcendent meaning, or with the historical revelance of the Christ, Tillich unavoidably runs into traditional Christian doctrines. These he reinterprets in order to assume them into his system. Whether his reinterpretations are orthodox or not is obviously an important question, but it is not the question to which Tillich primarily addresses himself: he does not "exclusively maintain a theology of revelation (as the neo-orthodox theologians have done)."[1]

Paul Tillich's attitude towards dogmas is explained at the beginning of *Systematic Theology* I. The first point that one notices is his reluctance to use the words "dogma" and "dogmatic." Tillich remarks that these expressions came to be used at a time when the Church was engaged in self-defence. The Creeds were adopted as a "protective formulation"[2] against heresies. Their acceptance became "a matter of life and death for Christianity."[3] This was a necessary step in the development of the Church, for heresies were demonic attempts to distort the Christian message. In this sense, a theology is always dogmatic: the "word 'dogmatics'

1. *Systematic Theology* I, p. 30.
2. *Ibid.*, p. 32.   3. *Ibid.*

emphasizes the importance of the formulated and officially acknowledged dogma for the work of the systematic theologian."[4] Yet Tillich shuns the word as much as possible, for he believes that the significance of dogmas became distorted after the first centuries. Instead of remaining protective formulations of the core of the Christian message, dogma was now identified with the laws of the Christian state. Heresy became a social crime. State and Churches that condoned this confusion became themselves demonic. There arose a demonic use of dogma, a reversal of values, by which dogmas were used, by "Catholic as well as Protestant, against theological honesty and scientific autonomy."[5] This unfortunate situation has "discredited the words 'dogmas' and 'dogmatics' to such a degree that it is hardly possible to re-establish their genuine meaning."[6]

Tillich's reluctance to use a vocabulary to which large sections of the intellectual world are allergic makes sense, for his purpose is precisely to build a bridge between the Christian faith and the secularized intellect. No antagonism to any specific dogma is implied. "This does not reduce the significance of the formulated *dogmata* . . . but it makes the use of the term 'dogmatics' impossible."[7] Paul Tillich must excuse the title of this chapter. We are trying to look critically at his theology from the standpoint of the believer, and this standpoint must remain dogmatic—whatever happens to scientific autonomy. The Christian is ultimately concerned about Christology, not only as symbol and as history, but also as dogma.

It is clear from the whole background of Tillich's theology that dogma itself, as he understands it, is a product, rather than a source, of theology. The ultimate source of Christian belief can only be the revelatory situation in which Jesus is perceived as the Christ. There are no "revealed dogmas" properly speaking, no *depositum* that was communicated to the Apostles and handed down through the life of the Church, to be infallibly taught to the faithful. Tillich's attitude is well epitomized in this sentence: "There are no revealed doctrines, but there are revelatory events

4. *Ibid.*   5. *Ibid.*
6. *Ibid.*   7. *Ibid.*

and situations which can be described in doctrinal terms."[8] Therefore, in seeking his view of the Christological dogmas, we are not following his analysis of Scripture or, perhaps, tradition, as the sources of Christian doctrine. This would be a Catholic method, and Tillich would have none of it. The concept of dogma as a *de fide* statement, and of dogmatics as an "exact and at the same time polemic interpretation" of dogma, is responsible for "the dogmatic sterility of Roman Catholic theology, in contrast to its liturgical and ethical creativity and the great scholarship it develops in areas of Church history which are free from dogmatic prohibitions."[9] Tillich is not too much impressed by any official endorsement of a dogma: dogma, as the formula covering an aspect of the revelatory event of Jesus as the Christ, was elaborated by theologians. It is always open to criticism by theologians in the light of their own participation in the same revelatory event. An official endorsement, by a Council for instance, is tremendously important for it shows that at one time in the history of the Church a certain dogma was perceived, by a responsible assembly, as necessary to safeguarding the faith, as indispensable to proclaiming the *kerygma*, yet it does not for ever hallow a particular formulation or dogma. Another period and another situation may require its abandonment, or make a radical re-interpretation imperative if we wish to preserve and to present the Christian message in that period and that situation.

The systematic theology that Tillich has built is essentially apologetic. Apologetics is not, for him, a part of theology: it is theology itself spanning the chasm between man and being-itself, showing to ultimately concerned man that the Christ has appeared in existence as the object of our ultimate concern. It is not apologetic in the sense of a defence of Christian teachings, revealed dogmas or theological propositions. We should therefore not expect Tillich to start from dogmatic statements. All he can do, while consistently working out the implications of his central theological position, is to investigate what meaning the traditional dogmas may or may not have in his system. The exact, primitive purpose of dogmatic statements is to be investigated as a matter of

8. *Ibid.*, p. 125.   9. *Ibid.*, p. 37.

historical information, but their original significance will not necessarily prevail in this new setting. Thus the starting-point of Tillich's theology gives him great freedom: the theologian no longer needs to bring his thought into line with traditional Christianity.

In other words, Tillich's attitude to dogmas, like his approach to the Bible, is one of demythologization. The Councils, and whatever other ecclesiastical authorities formulated the traditional dogmas, did but discover, in their apperception of the revelatory events of the Christ, symbols, or sets of symbols, pointing to the Christian message. This they formulated in propositions and rational statements. Combining these symbols, they constructed Christian myths. Thus the Creeds, with their picture of a divine being descending in the flesh and ascending to heaven again after passing through, and triumphing over, death, are mythological epics. Their truth does not lie in the historical exactness of every detail of the picture, but in the ability of those symbols to express the Unconditional appearing under the conditions of existence. Their value to the Church lasts as long as, and no longer than, their symbolic meaning is perceived. Dogmatic myths must be "broken," that is, understood symbolically. If we take them literally, we undermine their religious dimension. Creeds and dogmas then become intellectual taboos that must be defended without regard to scientific honesty.

Churches and theologians that see in Christianity a religion of authority and in dogmas immovable formulas endowed with infallibility naturally run foul of Tillich's liberal interpretation of the Creed. It is not that he denies authority to the Church; he only distinguishes it from an institutional authority. The Cross "is the greatest symbol of which I know for the true authority of the Church and the Bible. They should not point to themselves but to the reality which breaks again and again through the established forms of their authority."[10] The true God does not subject us "by divine order to an established religious authority as the earthly representative of his own heavenly authority."[11] Such authority would be *heteronomous*, corresponding to "the

10. *The New Being*, p. 88.   11. *Ibid.*, p. 89.

oppressive power of a heavenly tyrant."[12] Human rebellion against every authority would be *autonomous* and self-doomed. The only legitimate authority, be it that of the Church, of the Bible, or of the dogmas, is *theonomous*, in live continuity with the eternal and fathomless ground of our being, "a medium through which the Spiritual substance of our lives is preserved and protected and reborn."[13] The answer to the question of dogmatic authority is that Jesus established "an authority which cannot be established"; it is that "no answer can be given except the one that, beyond preliminary authorities, you must keep yourselves open to the power of him who is the ground and the negation of everything which is authority on earth and in Heaven."[14] If dogmas are authoritative, there is no ultimate authority except one that is beyond dogmas. If dogmas are opinions about God, they are only preliminary to ultimate concern about God: "You cannot have *opinion* about the Christ after you have faced him. You can only do the truth by following him, or do the lie by denying him."[15] Jesus the Christ is not, and neither the Church nor the theologian should be, "a teacher of truth among—or even above—other teachers of truth."[16] Once "broken," creedal myths and dogmatic statements are not "truths" comparable to others. They are not doctrines to be taught and learnt, but symbols to be experienced.

Paul Tillich's approach poses a serious question: How many Christological dogmas will survive such a treatment? We have already noted several points of traditional faith on which he has parted company both with Catholicism and with the Protestantism of the Reformers. I refer to the notion of faith,[17] the nature of original sin,[18] and the nature of revelation.[19] We have noticed that his description of the Cross omits the dogmatic statement that has hitherto inspired all Christian life and mysticism, namely that the Cross was the sacrifice of the Messiah to his Father.[20] We

12. *Ibid.*, p. 90.
13. *Ibid.*, p. 13.
14. *Ibid.*, p. 91.
15. *The Shaking of the Foundations*, p. 117.
16. *Ibid.*
17. Chapter III.
18. *Ibid.*
19. *Ibid.*
20. Chapter IV.

have further remarked that he underplays the historicity of the events that are basic to Christianity.[21] All this bodes ill for any fidelity to the traditional meaning of the Christian dogmas.

The central Christian dogmas are obviously those of the Incarnation and the Trinity. We have discussed Tillich's understanding of the Trinitarian dogma[22] but have deferred judgment on the orthodoxy of his Trinitarian theology pending further investigation of his Christology. Before examining his attitude towards the theology of the Incarnation, we shall first seek to appraise his identification of Jesus the Christ with the Word of God.

Father, Son, Spirit are symbols pointing to Being, Existence and Life in God. This is the sum total of Trinitarian thinking as Tillich explains it. All life is trinitarian, because it is the union of dynamic power with finite form. Since God is living, he must be thought of in trinitarian terms. In him there is Life, that is, there is Ground out of which Life springs, and there is Form in which Life expressed itself. Life is the union of Ground and Form, of Power and Limitation, of Infinity and Finiteness. The Ground is the Father; the Form is the *Logos*, or Son; the Life is the Spirit. The question raised by orthodox dogmatics concerns the interrelations of the three divine principles. Traditional theology as defined by the Councils of Nicaea and Constantinople is embodied in the Creed. It presents the Father, the Word and the Spirit as jointly one God, and distinctly three realities. The Church Fathers used various symbols to describe the oneness and the threeness of God. Little by little, the Church adopted "one substance (*ousia*) and three persons (*hupostasis*)" as expressing the orthodox faith. It thus steered a course between Tritheism (the division of the Trinity into three substances) and Sabellianism (the identification of Father, Son, Spirit with three aspects of God, without any real distinction). The creedal formulation of this is summarized in the word *homoousios* of the Council of Nicaea: the Word, though "born" of the Father, and therefore distinct from him, is nevertheless "of one substance" with him.

In Tillich's Trinitarian thinking, the *Logos* is also born of the

21. Chapter V.   22. Chapter IV.

Father. The Father is the eternal Abyss that becomes also Ground, Power to be, as the *Logos* rises. The *Logos* is of the substance of the Father: Abyss and Ground are one; the Depth of Being is also the Form of Being. Yet this is not orthodox. For the relation of the two as envisaged and explained by Tillich follows a Sabellian type. Father, Son and Spirit, or, in his vocabulary, Being, Existence and Life, or yet Abyss, Meaning and Unity, are aspects of being when being is conceived as living. They are, God as Infinite, God as Finite, God as uniting in himself finiteness and infinity. But these are not three realities in God. They are necessary distinctions if we accept the idea of the living God. The question is, Are these distinctions merely conceptual, or are they really distinct in God?

What puts us on the track of Sabellianism in Tillich's theology of the Trinity is that, far from answering the question, he never even asks it. This may not be enough to put a heretical label on him; but it is enough to show that he is not particularly interested in the question of a real versus a conceptual distinction between the Father, the Son and the Spirit. But this is not all. Described as "moments within the process of the divine life,"[23] the divine realities appear to be indistinguishable from their Sabellian or "Modalistic" description as aspects of God. In Tillich's theology our experience of the three aspects of life (power, structure and the unity of both) requires us to think of God in Trinitarian terms. Just as in us these three are only aspects and not distinct realities, so it would seem that Father, Son and Spirit are only aspects of our knowledge of God, which is exactly the Sabellian heresy.

Tillich himself gives us a hint in this direction when he minimizes the importance of describing the Word as *homoousios* with the Father. While acknowledging the necessity of this description "against the hero-cult of Arianism,"[24] he maintains that it resulted in a Christological confusion.[25] In *Systematic Theology* II, Tillich

---

23. *Systematic Theology* I, p. 250.
24. "A Reinterpretation of the Doctrine of the Incarnation," in *Church Quarterly Review* (London, England), No. 294, Jan.-March, 1949, p. 138.
25. *Ibid.*

finds the semi-Arian objection to *homoousios* rather congenial: "Only the God who is really God can create the New Being, not a half-god. It was the term *homoousios*, 'of equal essence,' which was supposed to express this idea. But in that case, the semi-Arians asked, how could a difference exist between the Father and the Son, and does not the picture of the Jesus of history become completely ununderstandable? It was hard for Athanasius and his most intimate followers (e.g., Marcellus) to answer such questions."[26] It seems very hard for Tillich, too. For he asserts again and again that a Christology based on *homoousios* sees the Christological problem as the problem of the two natures in Christ, that is, as "the dialectical relation of finiteness and infinity."[27] And this is an "impasse," a "Christology of absurdities." Why? Because "the starting point was wrong."[28]

From Trinitarian theology we have insensibly passed into Christology. Paul Tillich rightly notes that the two cannot be separated. If the Christ is the *Logos*, Christology implies Trinitarian thinking. One may therefore assume that, if Tillich's Trinitarian explanations do not fully satisfy the Christian dogma of the Trinity, this arises out of a faulty Christology. The orthodox Christology, as defined at the Council of Chalcedon, states the Christological question in terms of Incarnation: the "Word was made flesh" of the Gospel is interpreted as meaning that the Second Person of the Trinity, True God though he be, assumed the human nature and became man. In the Christ two natures, divine and human, were united in one divine Person.

Tillich's embarrassment with the doctrine of the Incarnation is patent. He himself admits it in words that are likely to leave the reader wondering: "I must confess that, in America, I have realized for the first time the importance of the concept of Incarnation, especially for the theology and liturgy of the Protestant Episcopal Church. But in spite of the religious and theological emphasis laid upon it, I find it difficult to find a clear and thorough

26. *Systematic Theology* II, p. 143.
27. "A Reinterpretation of the Doctrine of the Incarnation," p. 138.
28. *Ibid.*

interpretation of its meaning."[29] This confession was printed in 1949. How long it took Tillich to arrive at such a startling realization, we do not know. But it is amazing that a person who has been writing theological essays since the 1910's should have had to wait until his emigration to America in the 1930's to realize the importance of the doctrine of the Incarnation! Indeed we should be infinitely grateful to the Protestant Episcopal Church, if this realization came to Tillich through its mediation. Until then, he had written time and again that the problem of Christ must now be posited in terms of history, and not of nature. He had said that the doctrine of Chalcedon had become meaningless, and that we could not continue the old discussions about the two natures of Christ. Yet, though he has now realized the importance of the concept of the Incarnation, he is not satisfied with its meaning.

Tillich examines the doctrine of Chalcedon in two important studies. Having discovered the importance of the concept of Incarnation, Tillich tried to interpret it, or rather to reinterpret it. The frankest and, so it would seem to me, most unguarded expression of this attempt is an article in the (Anglican) *Church Quarterly Review*, precisely that article where he confessed his discovery of the importance of the concept. I call it unguarded, because Tillich attacks so many traditional views that one may wonder how far he is aware of his own iconoclasm. The other study appears in *Systematic Theology* II.

The first element that called for Tillich's attention was the necessary demythologization of the concept of Incarnation. "I became increasingly suspicious . . . that many people employed the concept of Incarnation in a mythological and superstitious manner: it implies for them the transmutation or metamorphosis of *a* divine being into *a* human being, a polytheistic myth which we find in all paganism; and incompatible with the fundamental truth of the prophetic revelation."[30] This, if it is found anywhere (which I am inclined to doubt), is a popular misconception of the Christian dogma. The Church has never said that "a" divine being became "a" human being. It says that "the Word was

29. *Ibid.*, p. 134.   30. *Ibid.*

made flesh" (St John) or that God the Son "was made man" (the Creed of Nicaea). But Tillich is not satisfied with throwing darts at popular misrepresentations; he proceeds to attack the Church dogma itself.

We have already seen Tillich having his doubts about the Trinitarian dogma of *homoousios*. This doubt is now extended to the doctrine of Chalcedon in the form of a downright denial. "The biblical interpretation of the Incarnation does not imply that God as such becomes man. . . . The statement is not that God becomes man. . . . The paradox of the Incarnation is not that God becomes man. . . . The proposition that God became man, or became flesh, is definitely not biblical."[31] Such a doctrine, if we are to believe Tillich, is not only unscriptural (a point which, given his methodological principles, is not absolutely essential), it is also absurd. For it involves theology in "the inescapable absurdities of the attempt to explain the Incarnation in terms of a higher chemistry between finiteness and infinity."[32]

Tillich's expression is somewhat inappropriate at this point (as when he likened Trinitarian theology to a "trick question" about the mutual compatibility of three and of one[33]), for no theology, and far less the dogma of Chalcedon about two natures in Christ, is a chemistry, but the exact opposite. It precisely avoids the confusion of God and man, the mixing up, in the manifestation of the Christ, of human and divine qualities. It guarantees that in Jesus, God is God and man is only man. Thus Monophysitism in all its forms is eschewed, and, because the two natures are united in one divine Person, so is Nestorianism: God and man in Christ are not two, but one. Apparently Tillich did not see, when he wrote these lines, the profundity of the concept of Incarnation.

What, then, did he see in the Incarnation? Jesus the Christ, in St Paul,[34] "is certainly not God himself, but a divine being."[35] Behind the mythological expressions of the New Testament, Tillich perceives "that a divine being, either the heavenly man, or the preexistent Christ, or the divine *Logos*, appears in the shape

31. *Ibid.*, pp. 134-39.   32. *Ibid.*, p. 139.
33. Chapter IV.   34. Phil. 2.5-11.
35. "A Reinterpretation of the Doctrine of the Incarnation," p. 135.

of a physical man or of a man in the flesh. . . . A divine being with human characteristics, the spiritual or heavenly man, or a moral being who chooses self-humiliation, or the creative reason and word, appears in time and space. . . . A divine being who represents God and is able to reveal him in his fullness, manifests himself in a form of existence which is in radical contradiction to his divine, spiritual and heavenly form."[36] The obvious question that comes to mind here is: What is a "divine being" if it is not God? Tillich has often insisted that there is no such thing as "a divine being," for this would imply a contradiction in terms. How can he now maintain that the Incarnation is just that: the appearance of "a divine being" who, we are told, is not God? For a solution he falls back on his analysis of myths: when he says that the Christ is a divine being, he means it symbolically. There is a mythological element here as in the Bible. Thanks to it, the doctrine of the Incarnation is understood "as the self-manifestation of God in existence through a divine half-being, half-principle which belongs to God, and nevertheless shows some essentially human characteristics."[37] The innocent reader is given the impression of a higher chemistry infinitely more confusing than the dogma of Chalcedon which, at least, is couched in intelligible terms. The myth of the Incarnation of a "half-being, half-principle," as reported by Tillich, is simply absurd.

Tillich, of course, does not rest there. One thing is to formulate a myth. Another is to "break" and explain it. What does the Incarnation myth mean? We are now on familiar ground again, for the Incarnation means what Tillich explains in all his Christological statements: "The Incarnation is the manifestation of original and essential Godmanhood within and under the conditions of existence."[38] When the "mythological, liturgical and numinous form" of Christological statements is translated "into a rational and theological form"[39] we obtain a simple enough scheme. Christianity "has a complete concept of man's essential nature, as well as of existence and of the radical contrast between them."[40] This essential nature appears in the picture of the Christ.

36. *Ibid.*, pp. 136-37.   37. *Ibid.*, p. 137.
3 8. *Ibid.*, p. 139.   39. *Ibid.*   40. *Ibid.*, p. 140.

In sharing its revelatory power we perceive "the New Being created by the Incarnation"[41]: it is "above essential being because it is actual and not merely potential; and at the same time, it is above existential being because it brings being or essential God-manhood into existence."[42] "It is essential humanity, and therefore essential Godmanhood which appears as New Being, above essence and existence."[43] The meaning of the Incarnation is, therefore, that in one biblical picture, the picture of the Christ, and at one historical moment, the Incarnation, the essence and the existence of man were reconciled. Then mankind was given a New Being, the Being which belongs to it in its essential Godmanhood, and yet which cannot be experienced under the conditions of existence. The paradox is that in the Christ essential Godmanhood was existentially experienced. "Essential Godmanhood has become historical Godmanhood in the man Jesus who is believed to be the Christ."[44]

The symbols of the Christ are symbols of an ontological victory, creating a New Being above the contradictions of essence and existence. Such is the meaning of the Incarnation for Tillich. As he himself says, "It offers a new approach to the interpretation of Jesus as the Christ."[45] At a former period of his development, Tillich insisted that the doctrine of the two natures could be meaningful now only if it was expressed in terms of history. This was the gist of *The Interpretation of History*, published in 1936. By 1949, the date of this epoch-making article on a "Reinterpretation of the Doctrine of the Incarnation," both the Chalcedonian positing of the problem and its "historical" reinterpretation were replaced by an ontological reinterpretation.

An orthodox Christian, be he Catholic or Protestant, can only judge Tillich's Christology in the light of the dogma of Chalcedon. At this point we must emphatically state that the Council of Chalcedon and Tillich's reinterpretation of the Incarnation are utterly incompatible. This will appear from Tillich's comments on Chalcedon in *Systematic Theology* II.

41. *Ibid.*, p. 142.   42. *Ibid.*
43. *Ibid.*, p. 144.   44. *Ibid.*   45. *Ibid.*, p. 146.

The dogma of Chalcedon is that in Jesus as the Christ, the human nature and the divine nature co-existed, and the human nature, soul and body, was actuated by the divine Person, the Word of God. Thus there was a real unity between the two natures of Christ while they both remained distinct, the one being merely human, undergoing all the tragedies of existence, sin excepted, the other being purely God. Tillich is convinced that the definition of this dogma was required as a safeguard against pagan distortions that would have seen Christ as a half-god: Christ had to be affirmed as fully divine. And it was also needed to counteract Monophysite tendencies, which would not have made Christ fully man. These are the two dangers that a Christology must avoid, and the two elements that it must protect. In Tillich's words, an attempt to express the mystery of Christ conceptually "can lead to an actual denial of the Christ-character of Jesus as the Christ; or it can lead to an actual denial of the Jesus-character of Jesus as the Christ. Christology must always find its way on the ridge between these two chasms."[46] The Christ-character of Christ refers to his divine dimensions; the Jesus-character to his human finitude. The dogma of Nicaea had begun solving the dilemma by identifying the Christ-character of Jesus with the eternal *Logos*. The dogma of Chalcedon continued in the same line: it described Jesus as having two natures, the human nature and the nature of the eternal *Logos*, expressed in the formula: two natures, human and divine, in the one divine *Persona* of the *Logos*.

This dogma was necessary and "saved the Church."[47] It has "substantial truth and historical significance."[48] Nevertheless, Tillich insists that the Nicene and Chalcedonian formulations ended in an "inescapable definitive failure."[49] The dogma of Chalcedon has "substantial truth" because in it "both the Christ-character and the Jesus-character of the event of Jesus as the Christ were preserved."[50] Yet it failed to formulate a definitive dogma, a dogma that would permanently protect the Church from error, because it used "very inadequate conceptual tools."[51]

46. *Systematic Theology* II, p. 142.   47. *Ibid.*, p. 140.   48. *Ibid.*, p. 142.
49. *Ibid.*   50. *Ibid.*, p. 145.   51. *Ibid.*

The concept to which Tillich objects in the Chalcedonian formula is the concept of nature. "The basic inadequacy lies in the term nature."[52] More specifically, "the term 'human nature' is ambiguous and the term 'divine nature' is wholly inadequate."[53]

Human nature, as Tillich understands it, refers to three elements in man. It refers to man's essence, to his estranged existence, or to "the ambiguous unity of the two."[54] As regards the Christ, the first and the third notions apply: Jesus was "man," and he was "involved in the tragic ambiguities of life"[55] for which the Cross stands as a symbol. As for the second notion, one must qualify Christ's participation in estrangement: "He has man's existential nature as a real possibility, but in such a way that temptation, which is the possibility, is always taken into the unity with God."[56] The word "nature" should therefore be qualified when applied to Christ: it cannot be used without distinctions and corrections. Tillich concludes: "Under these circumstances it is imperative to dismiss altogether the term 'human nature' in relation to the Christ and replace it by a description of the dynamics of life."[57] This I find a most extraordinary conclusion. In the first place, that the term "human nature" must be qualified when applied to Christ is certainly no reason to dismiss it, but only to qualify it. In the second place, I fail to see why a "description of the dynamics of life" could not be made while still speaking of the human nature of Christ. To describe the dynamics of life in Jesus is a most worthy attempt, and it by no means requires a rejection of the Chalcedonian description.

As to the expression "divine nature," "it cannot be applied to the Christ in any meaningful way; for the Christ (who is Jesus of Nazareth) is not beyond essence and existence."[58] The divine nature is, by definition, beyond essence and existence. If this is the nature of Christ, then Christ "could not be a personal life living in a limited period of time, having been born and having to die, being finite, tempted, and tragically involved in existence."[59] On account of this metaphysical impossibility, Tillich

52. *Ibid.*   53. *Ibid.*, p. 147.   54. *Ibid.*
55. *Ibid.*   56. *Ibid.*   57. *Ibid.*
58. *Ibid.*, p. 148.   59. *Ibid.*

finds the concept of divine nature, as applied to Christ, totally erroneous. But he has not noticed that this argument does not hit the dogma of Chalcedon, for it is Chalcedon that makes it impossible to confuse the human and the divine in Christ. What, in Christ, "is not beyond essence and existence" is the human element, the divine element remaining, by definition, beyond essence and existence. Tillich's point of departure disregards the Chalcedonian distinction, and it is on the strength of it that he denies the adequacy of the Chalcedonian formula. His reason for rejecting Chalcedon is, therefore, literally speaking, absurd: the premise is based on the conclusion; it takes for granted the opposite of what it tries to deny. Had Tillich paid more attention to the true meaning of the Chalcedonian Christology, he would have seen that his very starting-point is groundless, and he could not have denied Chalcedon on so shallow a basis. However, we must deal with what Tillich says, and not with what he should have said.

Tillich's assault on the Council of Chalcedon continues. Not only is the concept of two natures meaningless, but the union of the two natures in Christ remains, he believes, unexplained. The two natures "lie beside each other like blocks and [their] unity cannot be understood at all."[60] It cannot be understood simply because Tillich's exposition of Chalcedon pays so little attention to the concept of *hupostasis* or *persona*. The two natures are joined in what is called a "hypostatical union" by later theology. And it is remarkable that Tillich does not discuss this. Yet the Council of Chalcedon made clear how the two natures are united, namely, "in one person and one subsistence, not partitioned or divided in two persons, but in the one and self-same Son and only-born of God, the *Logos*, the Lord Jesus Christ."[61] The two natures are not "blocks": they are animated by one and the same centre of divine life, the Word of God. Because he has not perceived the depth of this unconfused union within the divine *Logos*, Tillich, "by eliminating the concept of two natures," wants to be "open to relational concepts which make

60. *Ibid.*
61. Denzinger, *Enchiridion Symbolorum*, n. 148.

understandable the dynamic picture of Jesus as the Christ."[62] This, too, is an amazing statement, for it is oblivious of the fact that, as it has been traditionally explained, the "person" of the Word, in which the two natures of Christ subsist, is itself a relational concept. The Word is a substantial relation to the Father. The Word also contains in himself the divine picture of all being. Created beings exist, precisely because they are related to their being-thought-by-God, that is, to the Word. In the case of Jesus, his created relation to the Word is, as it were, duplicated by the immediate presence of the Uncreated Relation to the Father, which is the eternal *Logos*. Jesus is perfectly man, and also perfectly the *Logos*. Thus the Chalcedonian formula provides a basis for a relational understanding of Jesus as the Christ, the very formula which Tillich wants to eliminate in order to develop a relational Christology! Once more his criticism of Chalcedon has veered around and destroyed itself.

Tillich's critical view of the Chalcedonian formula forms the weakest link in his Christology. It is not surprising that, having rejected the divine nature of Christ, which is now replaced by "eternal God-man-unity or eternal Godmanhood,"[63] he develops a slanted Trinitarian theology. The Christ is not God. He may be called divine because what he manifests is the eternal ground of being. The event of Jesus as the Christ remains unique. It is made possible by what it reveals, namely that there is "an eternal unity of God and man within the divine life."[64] For most men, this unity is a potentiality; it is, in our life, "actualized through finite freedom" and therefore ambiguously. On the contrary, in Jesus, the unity of God and man was actualized "against existential disruption"[65] in a triumph over ambiguity. The Christ submitted to, and conquered, the tragedy of existence. He thus manifested the New Being for which mankind had been longing. In terms of doctrine, what we can say of this unity of God and man in Christ is limited. "Abstract definitions of the nature of this unity are as impossible as psychological investigations into its character. One can only say that it is a community

62. *Systematic Theology* II, p. 148.   63. *Ibid.*
64. *Ibid.*   65. *Ibid.*

between God and the centre of a personal life which determines all utterances of this life and resists the attempts within existential estrangement to disrupt it."[66] In other words, one can describe Jesus as the Christ; one cannot explain him. The victory belongs to faith, perceiving the revelatory power of the Christ, not to philosophy or rational theology. To the question, What is the Christ? one can answer: He is the New Being, eternal Godmanhood manifested in existence. But to the question, Who is Christ? there is no answer. The Christ of history is hidden by two thousand years of piety and research. The Christ of faith is beyond historical or psychological investigation.

All this is in line with Tillich's article, "Reinterpretation of the Doctrine of the Incarnation." Between 1949 and 1957, the date of *Systematic Theology* II, his doctrine has not evolved. The criticism of Chalcedon has been made more precise, but the understanding of the Incarnation is the same. From the point of view of Christian orthodoxy, it is just as weak now as it was then.

No wonder that Tillich's Christology has been given heretical labels. Writing from a Roman Catholic position, Father Gustave Weigel, S.J., finds clear traces of Nestorianism in Paul Tillich's view of the Christ: "Tillichian Christology is Nestorian; nor would this label incommode Dr. Tillich, who sees much that is good in the doctrines of the Nestorian theologians."[67] Nestorianism, or what goes by that name, sees Christ as not only two natures, but also two persons. In Jesus there is a human person and the person of the divine *Logos*, not—as in the Chalcedonian formula—two natures in the divine person. Attributing such a view to Tillich would, at first sight, seem bold, considering his apparent rejection of the "two nature" doctrine. Yet Father Weigel clearly put his finger on a true strain in Tillich's thought, for Tillich himself declared this article to be "the best analysis of my thought I ever have seen."[68] Concerning the specific charge

66. *Ibid.*
67. Gustave Weigel, "Contemporaneous Protestantism and Paul Tillich" (*Theological Studies*, June, 1950), p. 194.
68. *Ibid.*, p. 201.

of Nestorianism, Tillich of course does not call himself a Nestorian. Yet he writes to Weigel: "You are further right that I am more in sympathy with the Antiochean rather than the Alexandrian Christology, although I have often been accused of Docetism, which is certainly nearer to Cyril than to Theodore."[69] Antiochean Christology, without being necessarily Nestorian, tends to emphasize the human element in Christ. Alexandrian theology, without being necessarily Monophysite, tends to stress the divine. The former is historically represented, among others, by Theodore of Mopsuestia, while the latter is represented by St Cyril of Alexandria. By accepting the appellation "Antiochean," Tillich wants above all to reject popular misconceptions of the doctrine of Chalcedon. Specifically he wants to oppose the notion of a pre-existing divine Being becoming Man. "If the *egeneto* in the Johannine sentence, *Logos sarx egeneto*, the Word was made flesh, is pressed, we are in the midst of a theology of metamorphosis."[70] We would be returning to a myth that Tillich has already exploded. It would mean that the Divine has become human, which is a contradiction. But Tillich's fears are groundless, for the doctrine of Chalcedon forms an effective barrier against such a conception: the *Logos* does not become human, he only assumes a human nature.

In order to shun the metamorphosis myth more surely, Paul Tillich favours an "adoptianist" Christology. And this is where he is, not only Antiochean, but openly Nestorian. In the original adoptianist theory, the man Jesus would, at some point in his career, have been adopted by God as his son. Without a concept of adoption, Tillich believes, Christ "would be deprived of his finite freedom; for a transmuted being does not have the freedom to be other than divine."[71] This indeed is a very bad reason to choose an adoptianist Christology, for the Chalcedon doctrine, once again, exorcizes the notion of a transmutation of God into a man much more effectively than adoptianism. Adoptianism certainly makes transmutation unthinkable with respect to the human elements in the Christ. But where is the divine element?

69. *Ibid.*, p. 202.   70. *Systematic Theology* II, p. 149.
71. *Ibid.*, p. 149.

Tillich retains it by attaching to his adoptianist Christology an "incarnational Christology."[72] "When Christianity uses the term 'Incarnation,' it tries to express the paradox that he who transcends the universe appears in it and under its conditions. In this sense every Christology is an incarnational Christology."[73] In Jesus as the Christ, the Jesus, being the human element, is adopted by God, while the Christ, being the manifestation of the ground of being, is divine, though he is not God. The two elements, human and transcendent, Jesus and Christ, are juxtaposed, instead of being, as at Chalcedon, organically united.

Writers who, like Father Weigel, have paid special attention to Tillich's view of Jesus, must therefore see it as Nestorian. Others, concentrating on Tillich's understanding of the Christ, consider his Christology as being Monophysite, or even Docetist. From the standpoint of a Protestant theology that comes close to the thought of Karl Barth, Maria Fuerth Sulzbach has scored Tillich's heterodoxy: "Tillich's ontology of the 'new being,' the basis of his theology, as far as it is Christological, is clearly indifferent toward all that the name 'Jesus' stands for. For Tillich the humanity of Jesus is unimportant."[74] To the "existentialism" of his analysis of the New Being, Tillich thus joins a form of Docetism. It is the New Being that matters; "it is more or less accidental that the personification of this idea took place in Jesus of Nazareth."[75] That the Word was made flesh is irrelevant. What matters is that the Apostles believed it and that, confronted by the biblical picture of the Christ, we still believe it.

We have seen that Tillich is not truly interested in the history of Jesus. At bottom, this is precisely because of an unavowed Docetism. Tillich ends up in a very strange position. Rejecting the pre-existence of the Christ as God, he insists on the human element in Jesus as the Christ. Then, turning his eyes to historical research, he despairs of reaching security there and abandons Jesus as Jesus. We may ask at this point: What is the human

72. *Ibid.*   73. *Ibid.*
74. Maria Fuerth Sulzbach, "The Place of Christology in Contemporary Protestantism" (*Religion in Life*, Winter, 1953-54), p. 212.
75. *Ibid.*

element in Jesus as the Christ, unless it is, precisely, Jesus as Jesus? Or, in the words of Maria Sulzbach, "Nowhere in the Gospels are there any testimonies to the effect that Jesus, the man, was at any given moment unimportant or less important than Jesus, the Christ."[76]

Our conclusion must therefore be unequivocal. Paul Tillich has failed to account for the biblical picture of Jesus and for the Christological dogma as the Church has always believed it. He has paid lip-service to the dogmas, by saying that "Protestant theology must accept the 'Catholic' tradition insofar as it is based on the substance of the two great decisions of the early Church, Nicaea and Chalcedon."[77] But when he himself tried "to find new forms in which the Christological substance of the past can be expressed,"[78] the Christological substance vanished. The divinity of Christ has been rejected for fear of a Christological metamorphosis. And the humanity of Christ has been declared unknowable. Thus both the Christ-character and the Jesus-character of Jesus the Christ have been lost. Where the Council of Chalcedon, spearheading the Church, follows a ridge between two chasms, the Christology of Paul Tillich falls into both chasms one after the other.

This conclusion does sound harsh. It is a far cry from what I myself wrote in 1953, when I said that I found in Paul Tillich no misinterpretation of the New Being in Jesus as the Christ.[79] The fateful article of 1949 on the "Reinterpretation of the Doctrine of the Incarnation" could still be charitably considered a freak. The publication in 1957 of Systematic Theology II made this reading of Tillich impossible. In trying to find his own way between orthodoxy and heterodoxy, he forgot that outside of orthodoxy there can only be heterodoxy. Orthodox Christology was formulated at Chalcedon. Every alteration of the Chalcedonian understanding of the Gospel is heterodox.

Before we finish with this topic, it may be good to test our

76. Ibid.   77. Systematic Theology II, 145.
78. Ibid., p. 145.
79. "The Unconditional Concern" (Thought, 1953), p. 244.

case again. Faith in the Resurrection of Christ has traditionally been a touchstone of orthodox Christology. Christ resurrected himself because, being God, he could do it; and he had occasion to rise from the dead only because, being fully man, he had died. The Resurrection is thus the biblical ground of the dogma of Chalcedon. Whoever disturbs the Chalcedonian balance must necessarily alter the scriptural data on the Resurrection.

According to Tillich the Resurrection is, with the Cross, a symbol illustrating the meaning of the central symbol of the Christ. Like the Cross, it is a combination of symbol and event. A certain event prompted the Apostles, in an ecstatic revelatory experience, to apply the symbol of the resurrection to Jesus as the Christ. "The certainty that he who is the bearer of the new eon cannot finally have succumbed to the powers of the old eon made the experience of the Resurrection the decisive test of the Christ-character of Jesus of Nazareth. A real experience made it possible to apply the known symbol of the resurrection to Jesus, thus acknowledging him definitely as the Christ."[80] The sequence of thought is clear. The symbol of the resurrection was, so to say, floating around in all the pagan religions at the time of Christ. Some event that was experienced by the Apostles convinced them that Christ, the New Being, had not yielded up his life to the final estrangement of death, in spite of the fact that he had been seen to die on the Cross. As a result of this event, the Apostles applied to him the religious symbol of the Resurrection: the Messiah had risen from the dead. This was part of the early *kerygma*, as witnessed by St Paul in 1 Corinthians 15. The Resurrection stories of the Gospels were elaborated later, not necessarily as factual descriptions of what happened, but rather as symbols of the triumph of Christ, the New Being, over death.

This may sound, so far, as a somewhat unusual presentation. Yet it is jejune enough. The Christian faith is obviously not committed to every detail in the Gospel records of the Resurrection. Faith is only committed to the Resurrection itself, as symbol and as event. "If Christ has not risen from the dead, vain is our faith"[81] is a thought echoed by Tillich. Though minimizing the

80. *Systematic Theology* II, p. 154.   81. 1 Cor. 15.17.

historicity of the New Testament, and referring to the Resurrection as only "a mysterious experience of a few,"[82] Tillich insists that "the factual element is a necessary implication of the symbol of the Resurrection."[83]

But the question arises as to what the mysterious event that gave rise to faith in the Resurrection of the Christ actually was. And it is here that Tillich's understanding of the Resurrection must be tested.

Tillich considers the usual three theories of the event of the Resurrection unsatisfactory. The first and "most primitive,"[84] he labels "physical." It is the story such as we find it in the Gospels. Christ arose, body and soul, from the sepulchre in which he had been buried. Tillich's comment is short and pungent: "Theologically speaking, it is a rationalization of the event, interpreting it with physical categories that identify resurrection with the presence or absence of a physical body. Then the absurd question arises as to what happened to the molecules which comprise the corpse of Jesus of Nazareth. Then absurdity becomes compounded into blasphemy."[85] In this way the understanding of the Resurrection which prevailed in all the Christian Churches until liberal Protestantism dissolved it is dismissed—and for the most extraordinary reason. Tillich speculates that "the sources of this story are rather late and questionable, and there is no indication of it in the earliest tradition concerning the event of the Resurrection, namely 1 Corinthians 15."[86] I am quite willing to accept Paul's reference as the earliest document that we have on this matter. But Paul is, *pace* Tillich, quite explicit as to the physical aspect of the Resurrection: "I delivered to you first what I had myself received, namely that Christ died for our sins according to the Scriptures, that he was buried, that he rose up on the third day according to the Scriptures, that he appeared to Cephas, and then to the twelve."[87] In specifying that Jesus the Christ rose from the sepulchre on the third day, Paul clearly alluded to an event that could be located (the tomb) and dated (the third day). The Gospel

---

82. *Systematic Theology* II, p. 153.   83. *Ibid.*, p. 155.
84. *Ibid.*   85. *Ibid.*, pp. 155-56.
86. *Ibid.*, p. 155.   87. 1 Cor. 15.3-5.

stories made the details more precise, but they added nothing substantial to what Paul knew of the original event of the Resurrection: Christ rose from the tomb on the third day. This can obviously only mean that he rose with his own body. That such was the meaning intended by Paul is clear from the argumentation of Chapter 15: the Resurrection of Christ is unique in that it is the first resurrection, but our own resurrection will be modelled on it: "Christ has risen from the dead, the first fruits of those who have been asleep."[88] The physical resurrection of the body of Jesus is then not, as Tillich suggests, "absurdity" and "blasphemy." It is the very cornerstone of the Christian faith.

Two other theories of the Resurrection can be briefly dismissed. They are not very serious, being neither biblical nor traditional. One of these sees the Resurrection as a "spiritualistic" phenomenon: only the soul of Jesus rose from the dead. It made itself felt somehow by the disciples. Tillich rightly says that this "cannot explain the factual side of the Resurrection of the Christ symbolized as the reappearance of the total personality, which includes the bodily expression of his being."[89] A third theory is "psychological" and sees the Resurrection as "an event in the minds of Jesus' adherents."[90] Tillich comments: "The psychological theory misses the reality of the event which is presupposed in the symbol—the event of the Resurrection of the Christ."[91]

Having thus left "physical or spiritualistic literalists"[92] to their delusions, Tillich seeks a different solution. I must acknowledge that he presents his theory with the utmost prudence. He offers it as a theory, which "is most adequate to the facts," but "does not have the certainty of faith."[93] He hopes, however, that literalists who reject it will nevertheless acknowledge that this story is justified by "the attitude of the New Testament and especially of the non-literalistic Apostle Paul."[94]

This "restitution theory," as Tillich calls it, holds that Jesus of Nazareth never rose bodily from the tomb. The Resurrection has nothing to do with the presence or the absence of a body.

88. 1 Cor. 15.20.
90. *Ibid.*
92. *Ibid.*, p. 158.
89. *Systematic Theology* II, p. 156.
91. *Ibid.*
93. *Ibid.*
94. *Ibid.*

It has to do with the continuing power of the Christ as the New Being, even after the death and burial of Jesus. The disciples realized that Jesus was dead, and yet they knew that, being the Christ, the New Being, he must have power beyond death. "In this tension something unique happened. In an ecstatic experience the concrete picture of Jesus of Nazareth became indissolubly united with the reality of the New Being."[95] The New Being is experienced by the Apostles in spite of the death of Jesus. They are still totally committed to the Christ, even though, during the Passion, they despaired of Jesus. In this continuing revelatory experience of the New Being, they restituted to Jesus the power of the Christ. They realized that Jesus was still present, not indeed in the "character of a revived (and transmuted) body . . . nor of the reappearance of an individual soul." It was a spiritual presence: "He 'is the Spirit' and we 'know him now' only because he is the Spirit. In this way the concrete individual life of the man Jesus of Nazareth is raised above transitoriness into the eternal presence of God as Spirit."[96] This "restitution of Jesus as the Christ," this "restitution of Jesus to the dignity of the Christ in the minds of the disciples,"[97] is the original event which justified the application to Jesus of the Resurrection symbol.

The trouble is that this theory does not do justice to St Paul. Jesus was not understood to be still the Christ in spite of his body lying in the tomb. He was understood to have risen from the tomb "on the third day." To say this is neither absurd nor blasphemous. It is the apostolic faith. The absurdity would be to believe that the Apostles accepted the Resurrection stories and the fact of the rising from the tomb while knowing perfectly well that Jesus had not risen from the tomb and had not resurrected in his own body. The myth of the Resurrection makes no sense unless it refers to a bodily resurrection. I would have been much simpler to say that Christ was still present as Spirit, if this is what the Apostles experienced, than to invent a Resurrection myth which they knew would be taken literally and would therefore mislead people. There was no point in delivering to others

95. *Ibid.*   96. *Ibid.*, p. 157.
97. *Ibid.*

the faith that "the Christ was buried and that he rose on the third day," if they only experienced his spiritual presence. This, indeed, would have been an absurdity and a blasphemy.

Paul Tillich's theory of the Resurrection of Jesus is in keeping with this departure from the faith of Chalcedon. There would be little basis for a resurrection of Christ in the flesh, if God had not been incarnated in the flesh. Having renounced the Incarnation, and yet desiring to keep the symbol of the Resurrection, Tillich had to find a theory that would preserve the symbol while emptying it of its reference to the flesh. If Tillich was not entirely a Docete in denying the two natures of Christ, he became one in describing the Resurrection. Rejection of the faith of Chalcedon thus had its expected consequences. A disturbance of the analogy of faith on one point is bound to echo through the entire structure. Tillich's previous abandonment of the orthodox understanding of the Incarnation led to his denying the Resurrection of the body of Jesus.

I would not like to end this chapter on the bugle-sounding of a heresy-hunter. After this lengthy examination of Tillich's understanding of the Christological dogma, I have no doubt that his theology is, on this matter, heretical. It is unbiblical. It is not in keeping with the traditional formulations of the early Councils. It is incompatible with the theology of the Fathers and that of the medieval Doctors. It is irreconcilable with the faith of the Protestant Reformers in the sixteenth century. In our century it appears as an outgrowth of liberal Protestantism, substituting an ontological principle for the latter's moral emphasis. To be sure, it appeals powerfully to those who, without being too scrupulous about the sources of the Christian faith, wish to absorb the existential emphasis of modern philosophy.

Having formerly taken a very favourable view of Tillich's theology of Unconditional Concern, I may perhaps be permitted these critical remarks without being accused of prejudice and blind hostility.

But I have not only critical remarks to make. I have attacked Tillich's theological theories concerning the Christological dogma and the Resurrection. I have also exposed his departure from traditional Christianity on other basic dogmas and theological positions. But I have not touched his faith. From reading the two volumes of sermons, *The Shaking of the Foundations* and *The New Being*, I feel sure that Paul Tillich's faith is Christian, if Protestant Christian, even though I fear that his theology, as expounded in *Systematic Theology* II, is not. For instance, one cannot read his sermon "Born in the Grave" without being caught in what Tillich would call a revelatory experience.

> It is the same subject, Jesus Christ, of whom it is said that he suffered and that he was buried and that he was resurrected. . . . Only the Messiah can bring birth out of death. It is not a natural event. It does not happen every day, but it happens on the day of the Messiah. . . . The Christ *must* be buried in order to be the Christ, namely, he who has conquered death. . . . The answer of Easter has become possible precisely because the Christ has been buried. The new life would not really be *new* life if it did not come from the complete end of the old life. Otherwise, it would have to be buried again. But if the new life has come out of the grave, then the Messiah himself has appeared.[98]

Or let us take the sermon called "Universal Salvation":

> Since the hour when Jesus uttered a loud cry and breathed his last and the rocks split, the earth ceased to be the foundation of what we build on her. Only in so far as it has deeper ground, can it stand; only in so far as it is rooted in the same foundation in which the Cross is rooted, can it last. And the earth not only ceases to be the solid ground of life; she also ceases to be the lasting cave of death. Resurrection is not something added to the death of him who is the Christ; but it is implied in his death. . . . No longer is the universe subjected to a higher law, to the law of life out of death by the death of him who represented eternal life. The tombs were opened and bodies were raised when one man in whom God was present without limits committed his spirit into his Father's hands. . . .[99]

98. *The Shaking of the Foundations*, pp. 166–68.
99. *The New Being*, pp. 178–79.

Through these lines, and many others in Tillich's sermons, we are grasped by the Power of Jesus the Christ, who has ushered in the new eon, who has translated us to the New Being. Such a deep commitment to Jesus the Christ ought not to have been marred by a misunderstanding of the Christian dogmas and an infidelity to some parts of the apostolic message and some of the traditional formulations of faith. But, while recognizing the many misconceptions in his theology, one must also acknowledge the unmistakable ring of self-commitment in his sermons. Tillich as preacher is infinitely more faithful to the Word than Tillich as system-builder.

Chapter VII

CHRISTOLOGY AS ETHICS

IN his introduction to *Systematic Theology*, Paul Tillich briefly discusses the place of ethics in a theological system. As against the theologians of the scholastic period of Protestant theology, he agrees with Karl Barth and neo-orthodoxy that ethics cannot be meaningfully separated from dogmatics. "The ethical element is a necessary—and often predominant—element in every theological statement."[1] His system contains no separate category for ethical problems. From beginning to end everything is ethical by implication. However, two sections of *Systematic Theology*, not yet published, are bound to deal more explicitly with ethical questions: a section on the Spirit, involving a study of moral and spiritual life, and another on the Church and the Christians, which must bring into focus society and personality. Still, since every theological statement is also ethical, there is no reason for believing that the third volume of *Systematic Theology* will reveal anything that has not already been suggested in Tillich's previous works. For instance, the notion of sin must be affected by the explanation of original sin contained in Vol. II: if original sin is simply man's necessary passage from essence to existence, sin can no longer be understood in terms of disobedience to a law.

Tillich's Christology stands out among those of his theological tenets that modify generally accepted concepts of Christian ethics. All of his thought hinges on a reinterpretation of Christology in ontological terms. Ethics must then undergo a parallel reinterpretation. Morality is illumined in new and perhaps unexpected ways by the Christology of the New Being. Once faith is understood as Ultimate Concern, as commitment to the Unconditional, a new ethical dimension is disclosed. No concern would be ultimate or unconditional if it did not determine the entire

1. *Systematic Theology* I, 31.

range of man's activities. Nothing can escape its influence if it is truly unconditional. The search for the Christ in the ambiguities of life is also a quest for the transformation of guilt into justice and love. The dogma that Christ's death atoned for our sins is, in Tillich's perspective, symbolic of the ethical dimension of faith in the New Being. The New Being in the Christ is redeemed. It has risen above the equivocation of the desire for holiness and the inevitability of temptation.

The correlation between ontology and ethics is indicated briefly in *The Religious Situation*: the question about ethics is "the question about activity directed toward the Unconditional."[2] The question is not, simply, one of behaviour. Behaviour and its conformity to a standard are inseparable from an ethics of law, but Tillich's background is Lutheran, and Luther emphasized the difference between Law and Gospel. St Paul's words on the shortcomings of the Torah have been applied, by Lutheran theology, to any expression of New Testament ethics in terms of law. Consequently, such an ethics, be it natural or revealed, is repugnant to Protestant moralists. Morality is treated in terms of love rather than of law. Obedience to any law fosters self-righteousness because it stresses the merits of good works rather than undeserved grace. In viewing ethics as the relationship of man's activity to the Unconditional, Tillich remains faithful to a basic Lutheran theme.

Accordingly, he shies away from defining a system of morality. He knows that many such systems have been constructed, both inside and outside religion. But to define some actions as good and others as bad is, he says, to forget one point. Life is not only creativity; it is also destructiveness. "Every life-process unites a trend towards separation with a trend towards reunion."[3] So does moral life. There is no good action without renunciation of a better one. Not only is evil exclusive of good; good itself is exclusive of better. In other words, good and evil are only relative values. An objective ethics, that claims absoluteness for its categories, is misleading. The lasting element of any code of morality is not to be found in its classification of good and of bad. Rather, ethics is valuable through its relationship to the Un-

2. *The Religious Situation*, p. 150.   3. *Systematic Theology* I, p. 279.

conditional. Because of this there can be, ultimately, no secular ethics. "An ethics can come to fulfilment only as a religious ethics."[4] The quest for salvation and morality is not a quest for a law, but for transcendence above all law. It is a quest for a paradoxical reconciliation of creativity and destructiveness in life, for a harmony of better, good and evil. The answer to the moral question is not moral; it is, in Tillich's phrase, "transmoral."

If Tillich exorcizes objective ethics from the start, he is equally distrustful of subjective ethics. Morality cannot be reduced to anyone's subjectivity, for this would ignore "the unconditional demand of the other person."[5] The Unconditional which we recognize in the experience of the New Being in Christ must be acknowledged not only in ourselves but also in other human beings, or it "would be an illusion."[6] The ethical realm of personal behaviour must be transcended in an attitude that embraces the Unconditional both in myself and in all others. "There is no depth of life without the depth of the common life."[7] Thus, the quest for morality arises as a search for "the unity of the personal and the Unconditional, or of the ethical and the religious."[8]

The ethics of the New Being is neither objective nor subjective. It must transcend subjectivity and objectivity. The only human experience in which both are transcended, because they are united in a higher synthesis, is love. Ultimately, therefore, Christian ethics must be an ethics of love.

These preliminary remarks have introduced us to the core of Christology in its ethical dimension. The Lutheran dialectic of Law and Gospel, the transcendence of good and bad, and the activity directed towards the Ultimate, are but aspects of one principle, the principle of the Protestant protest, of justification by faith alone through grace alone. And this, as we know, constitutes the heart of Tillich's interpretation of Christology.

The scholastics wrote of moral problems in terms of *De Conscientia* and *De Lege*. The treatise on conscience safeguarded

---

4. *The Religious Situation*, p. 153.   5. *The Protestant Era*, p. 216.
6. *Ibid*.   7. *The Shaking of the Foundations*, p. 57.
8. *The Protestant Era*, p. 216.

the necessary subjective part of responsibility. The treatise on law maintained the objective aspect of moral obligation. Contrary to what may be inferred from the term "law," the law to which the scholastics subordinated conscience was not a set of commands and prohibitions. It was a dynamic concept: the law is God's own rule for man to follow. Having presided over creation, this law left its mark on man's nature. Being itself an aspect of the Word of God, it was confirmed by the Incarnation. Revealed law, in this line of thought, is not superadded to the law of nature. Rather, it opens man's nature to the full meaning of the law.

Tillich is acquainted with Catholic ethics. Viewing it from the standpoint of the relationships of ethics to changing historical situations, he dubs it a "static supra-naturalistic solution."[9] As he understands it, Catholic ethics centres on the affirmation of eternal ethical structures. These immovable norms, "performed in the divine mind," correspond to the essence of created beings. Because of this, "the norms and laws for man's personal practice" must be patterned on them. Existence in man tries to mould itself on essence as it is thought out in God. The universe is therefore a hierarchy of values on the model of the eternal laws in God's mind. Between the universe and God, between existence and essence, the Church mediates: "The Church, itself a hierarchical system, teaches this system, educates for it, fights for its political realization, defends it against new systems." Although Tillich has called this a "static" solution to the ethical problem, he is well aware of the underlying dynamics: the Church "adapts its ethical system to the new problems and new demands. The Catholic Church has been able to do so in an admirable way for centuries, and the living authority of the pope is still a marvellous instrument for achieving adaptations without losing its immovable basis."[10] Nonetheless, he believes that the ethical system of Catholicism has failed to adapt itself to the modern world. The spirit of modern society has been uninfluenced by "the important utterances of the Holy See during the nineteenth century concerning social and political problems."[11] This failure is due, precisely, to what Tillich sees as a static element in Catholic

9. *Ibid.*, p. 151.   10. *Ibid.*   11. *Ibid.*, p. 152.

ethical thinking. The supra-naturalistic element in it corresponds to the concept of the eternal law. The static element corresponds to the static notion of the Church that Catholicism maintains. The Church, mediating between man and the divine law, is influential as long as "the unbroken unity and authority of the Christian Church, which no longer exists,"[12] is preserved. Since the Reformation and the breakdown of unity and authority, the situation has changed; yet the Catholic Church, Tillich thinks, has refused to recognize this change. As a result, the Catholic ethical system is powerless outside of the institutional limits of Roman Catholicism. It no longer has universal application. It does not reach even as far as Christianity.

Tillich's universe knows of no earthly, small-scale, model of the eternal law. God's rule for man to follow is not expressed in anything permanent, whether Church or Bible. Catholic ethics has succumbed to the permanent danger that threatens Christian moralists, that of "abusing Jesus by stating that he is the founder of a new religion, and the bringer of another, more refined, and more enslaving, law."[13] For "perfectionists, puritans and moralists,"[14] Jesus becomes "a teacher of the religious law, putting upon us the heaviest of all burdens, the burden of *his* law."[15] Had Jesus done this, he would have failed to be the Christ. Instead of manifesting the eternal ground of the Protestant principle, he would have contradicted it. All systems of ethics, Christian or otherwise, be they "static supra-naturalistic," like Catholicism, "dynamic naturalistic," like Nazism, or "rationalistic progressive," like Anglo-Saxon philosophy,[16] ultimately run foul of the principle of justification by faith alone. Man is not, and cannot be, justified by anything of his own doing; he is not, and cannot be, separated from God by his sinful actions: sinful or not in his behaviour, he always is estranged from God. What stands in the way of the divine is not his bad deeds only; it is his very existence. "The self, as such, is sinful before any act; it is separated from God, unwilling to love him."[17] This is existential estrange-

12. *Ibid.*   13. *The Shaking of the Foundations*, p. 99.
14. *Ibid.*, p. 98.   15. *Ibid.*
16. *The Protestant Era*, p. 151.   17. *Ibid.*, p. 146.

ment as we find it described at length in *Systematic Theology* II.

The Protestant principle, as Tillich understands it, is the end of all law, for every law stands in judgment under it. Because this has not been adequately perceived, "we see in all Christian Churches the toiling and labouring of people who are called Christians, serious Christians, under innumerable laws which they cannot fulfil, from which they flee, to which they return, or which they replace by other laws. This is the yoke from which Jesus liberates us."[18] To those who come to Christianity, on the contrary, one should proclaim the principle that none of their good deeds has ultimate value before God and that none of their bad deeds is ultimately damning: "Forget your Christian morals, your achievements and your failures, when you come to him. Nothing is demanded of you—no idea of God, and no goodness in yourselves, not your being religious, not your being Christian, not your being wise and not your being moral."[19] The ethics of the New Being perceives good in evil just as the ontology of the New Being sees faith in unbelief. A law defines good and evil; it imposes commands and prohibits certain acts. But two distinct attitudes can be opposed to that. Immoralists take the opposite of the law, calling evil good and good evil. The Christian attitude which Tillich advocates sets moralists and immoralists back to back, proclaiming a plague on both their houses. The ethics of the New Being is neither a law, nor lawlessness. It is ecstatic. It perceives, in the power of a revelatory situation, that both good and evil are self-condemned for they are both self-centred. "We call Jesus the Christ not because he brought a new religion, but because he is the end of religion, above religion and irreligion, above Christianity and non-Christianity."[20] The New Being manifested in the Christ is also above morality and immorality. It demands nothing but "your being open and willing to accept what is given to you, the New Being, the being of love and justice and truth, as it is manifest in him whose yoke is easy and whose burden is light."[20a] The morality of the Christ does not mean that we can be saved by good actions or damned by evil actions; it

18. *The Shaking of the Foundations*, p. 99.
19. *Ibid.*, p. 102.   20. *Ibid.*   20a. *Ibid.*

means that "there is a creative and saving possibility implied in every situation, which cannot be destroyed by any event."[21] Deep under the estrangement from God which is our existence and which our life manifests, there lies a unity, a unity with the ground of being, with the power to be. The ethics of the New Being consists in letting the power to be inform all our actions. The forgiveness of sins of the Gospels is a symbol of this victory of the ground of being over existence; it conveys "the certainty that we reach eternal life in spite of suffering and sin."[22]

In the light of the Protestant principle, then, a saving act is an act in which we are ultimately concerned. No man can make a moral judgment. None can decide that an act is good and another evil. The only ultimate evil is the denial of the ground of being. This does not mean that the ethics envisaged by Paul Tillich completely ignores commands and prohibitions, but no commands and prohibitions necessarily follow upon the perception of the New Being. In practice, the contents of ethics are a cultural phenomenon. Laws and interdicts are borrowed from spontaneous assumptions in the development of civilization. Christian revelation does not give a new law and a new set of commands; it gives a new spirit, in which any law may be accepted as a norm of behaviour because it is already transcended in spirit.

This is tantamount to saying that the solution of the moral question is not *moral*. In *The Protestant Era* Tillich asks: "Can the problem of conscience be answered at all in terms of *moral* conscience?"[23] His answer is negative. The ultimate solution of the problem of conscience lies beyond morals. Morality itself is only a question. The answer is provided in the "transmoral conscience."[24] The quest for the New Being is also a quest for a transmoral conscience. We find ourselves on familiar ground here. Tillich has already sought for a theonomy that would be beyond autonomy and heteronomy. Immorality is autonomous; and morality is heteronomous. There must be a theonomous ethics in which man is neither caught in the fallacy of autonomy nor made to groan under the demonic claims of laws.

21. *Ibid.*, p. 106.   22. *Ibid.*, p. 107.
23. *The Protestant Era*, p. 145.   24. *Ibid.*

Paul Tillich is convinced that the transmoral character of the ethics of the New Being is not a theoretical construction on his part; it does not only follow from a rigorous analysis of the implications of the Protestant principle. His book *Biblical Religion and the Search for Ultimate Reality* expresses the belief that the ethics of the Old and the New Testaments is not an ethics of law and sin, but of transcendence above obedience and disobedience.

The Bible presents man's existence in relation to God as being, "above all, ethical existence."[25] The Law of Moses emphasizes the ethical elements of existence. Tradition weighted it in the direction of heteronomy; but the prophetic protest against formalism restored the balance. The ethics of the Old Testament is thus in a constant tension between law and prophecy, between fear and love. In the New Testament, "Jesus reinterprets the law, shows its radical implications, and sums it up in the commandment of love."[26] If we really "expose ourselves to the overwhelming weight of ethical material in biblical religion . . . we should be aware of the way in which biblical personalism deals with ethics."[27] The idea that the human part in the Covenant with God is the fulfilment of the law saves biblical ethics from legalism. When the Alliance was understood in its depth, the law did not appear as "a system of virtues and vices, of laws and counsels, of rewards and punishments."[28] Rather, it helped define the concrete situation in which man had to make his choice, "for or against Yahweh, for or against the Christ, for or against the Kingdom of God."[29] Commands were always prominent; prohibitions were enforced; counsels were intended to be taken with deadly seriousness. But the basic element was elsewhere. Commands, prohibitions and counsels were concrete embodiments of the polarity of ultimate agreement or ultimate rejection. "Every decision is urgent; it has to be made now. When it has been made, it has far-reaching consequences. It is always an ultimate decision—a decision of infinite weight."[30] The system of biblical ethics, with its laws and practices extending to all fields of

25. *Biblical Religion and the Search for Ultimate Reality*, p. 44. 26. *Ibid.*
27. *Ibid.*, p. 45. 28. *Ibid.*
29. *Ibid.* 30. *Ibid.*

life and regulating, in the Pharisaic tradition, every minute of the day, is only meant to emphasize the seriousness of the ethical decision and its ultimacy.

Decision means choice. What ethical choice does the Bible propose? "Every generation in every nation has to decide for or against righteousness, for or against him who is the God of righteousness. And in every nation, including the selected one, the decision against righteousness means self-destruction."[31] This only pushes the problem further back, for what is righteousness? It is not the fulfilling of a law or the doing of a good deed. It is not the acquiring of merits or the avoiding of sins. It is, in the light of the Protestant principle, acknowledging with ultimate seriousness that all righteousness is from God and not from man. To choose the righteousness that is from God is to choose the Christ. To prefer a righteousness that would be from man is to decide against the Christ.

What of those who do not know the Christ or who have never been explicitly told that true righteousness is from God? Paul Tillich notes that in most cases "the decision for or against the Christ is made by people who do not even know his name."[32] But this does not invalidate his conception of the ultimate ethical question as he abstracts it from biblical ethics. "What is decisive is only whether they act for or against the law of love, for which Christ stands. Acting according to it means being received in the unity of fulfilment. Acting against it means being excluded from fulfilment and being cast into the despair of non-being. This is biblical ethics."[33] From this standpoint, biblical ethics means being presented with an ultimate choice and making with courage an ultimate decision. In every such choice the fight of light with chaos, of Christ with estrangement, is fought anew. And in every choice of absolute love the victory of the New Being over estrangement and existence triumphs again. Obviously, this "has little to do with the middle-class ethics of avoiding a few things which are supposed to be wrong, and doing a few things which are supposed to be right."[34] As Paul Tillich reads it, the

31. *Ibid.*   32. *Ibid.*, p. 46.
33. *Ibid.*   34. *Ibid.*

Bible thus posits the question of a way beyond morality and immorality, on the outer side of obedience and disobedience. Once more we meet the problem of the transmoral conscience.

In his *The Protestant Era* Tillich describes the transmoral conscience as superseding modern philosophical theories of conscience. Tillich, who has his biblical moods, more frequently has philosophical moods. In both cases the contents of his doctrine are the same. It is the presentation that differs. Philosophically speaking, the idea of the transmoral conscience springs from the difficulties of what Tillich calls the "emotional-esthetic," the "abstract-formalistic," and the "rational-idealistic" interpretations of conscience. The first rests on the principle of a universal harmony which man discovers through his conscience, and with which he should harmonize his actions. Tillich attributes it to Shaftesbury, Hume and Adam Smith. The second, represented by Kant in philosophy and Ritschl in theology, and exploited by Fichte, sees the conscience as an obligation without specific object. In both cases there was an attempt to rise above heteronomy in the direction of a transmoral conscience. But the attempt was foiled, in the first case, by "the revolutionary morality and immorality of the twentieth century,"[35] in the second, by the "loss of a concrete direction of conscientiousness," which paved the way for "very immoral contents" in the totalitarian state.[36] The third theory, attributed to Thomas Reid and present in the works of Hegel and Max Scheler, tries to unite "rationality and content."[37] While avoiding subjectivity, it fails to develop a satisfactory ethics because it defines the contents of conscience according to an exterior principle such as the State with Hegel, or the Church with Scheler. A correct approach to ethics would make conscience subservient neither to a formal content nor to an exterior source of obligation.

Such, precisely, is the transmoral conscience. "A conscience may be called 'transmoral' which judges, not in obedience to a moral law, but according to the participation in a reality which tran-

35. *The Protestant Era*, p. 143.   36. *Ibid.*, p. 36.
37. *Ibid.*, p. 144.

scends the sphere of moral commands."[38] Tillich ascribes to Luther the derivation of "a new concept of conscience from the experience of justification through faith."[39] Along this line the theology of the transmoral conscience was bound to arise. Justification through faith is an ultimate experience which throws new light on all things, including the commands of morality. "Justification by grace, in Luther's sense, means the creation of a transmoral conscience."[40] We know what this means. Justification implies that it is "not because of our moral perfection but in spite of our moral imperfection [that] we are fighting and triumphing on the side of God."[41] We are justified in our estrangement and sin. In the experience of sin we are graciously justified. Participation in the New Being is the other side of the experience of estrangement. It is the depth of estrangement, the abyss and the ground under existence. Man's actions, whether good or bad, reveal, in the ecstatic experience of the New Being in the Christ, an ultimate ground: the saving grace of the courage to be, the universal redeeming power of being-itself. The ethical question is not, to do or not to do; it is, to be or not to be, to accept or to reject being-itself.

The transmoral conscience, however, is not without content. It is rooted in the power to be. It is enlightened by the historical manifestation of the power to be under the conditions of existence in Jesus the Christ. On the strength of this, the transmoral conscience dominates all law and all morality. "It determines a situation instead of being determined by it."[42] If it is not, in this sense, moral, neither is it amoral or immoral. For its very definite content is immovable, being no other than the ultimate rock of life, justification of the sinner: "*The good, transmoral conscience consists in the acceptance of the bad, moral conscience*, which is unavoidable wherever decisions are made and acts performed."[43] That is to say, as soon as man acts ethically, he develops a moral conscience, a system of good and evil, categories of good deeds and misdeeds. It matters little where the contents of this moral

38. *Ibid.*, p. 145.   39. *Ibid.*
40. *Ibid.*, p. 146.   41. *Ibid.*
42. *Ibid.*, p. 148.   43. *Ibid.*

conscience come from. They may derive from religion or from society; they may be biblical commands, primitive taboos, bourgeois prejudices, or superstitions. What matters is that the moral conscience, judging itself in the light of the New Being, perceives its incapacity to do justice to being-itself even in its fulfilment of an accepted system of ethics. Then, "it is impossible *not* to transcend the moral conscience because it is impossible to unite a *sensitive* and a *good* conscience."[44] The content of the transmoral conscience consists therefore in accepting both the dictates of the moral conscience and also the guilt that unavoidably accompanies ethical action, in the knowledge that even morality does not justify. "The moral conscience drives beyond the sphere in which it is valid to the sphere from which it must receive its conditional validity."[45] The moral conscience receives its validity from the ecstatic perception of its incapacity: when this takes place, the transmoral conscience is born. It is the ethical analogue of faith as the self-transcendence of the intellect.

What the transmoral conscience brings is neither security nor comfort. The man who is justified does not cease to be a sinner, and there is no comfort in accepting life in a boundary-situation, on the boundary-line that forms a ridge between and above the affirmations and the negations of morality. "If we accept the message of the new reality in the Christ, we must understand that this message does not contain an easy answer, and that it does not guarantee spiritual security."[46] The transmoral conscience does not prescind from the human situation; on the contrary, it knows that there is no ultimate answer to the ethical question unless we experience it "permanently in the light of our human situation, in which tragedy and hope fight each other without victory."[47] It is the meaning of the Cross that victory is given in death, that resurrection is also crucifixion. The New Being arises out of the wreck of the old being. Then there is no security; there still is sin and guilt, estrangement and frustration. But there is liberty. For sin and guilt, estrangement and frustration are accepted as revelatory of the ground of all being. "Bond-age and fear have disappeared; obedience has ceased to be obedience and has become free inclination; ego and super-ego are united. This is the liberty of the children of God, liberty from the law, and because from the law, also from the condemnation to despair."[48]

With liberty, holiness is recovered. The holy is man's apprehension of the divine. When a man commits himself unreservedly to the New Being, he enters into communion with God. In a morality of command and prohibition, "the holy loses its depth, its mystery, its numinous character."[49] When morality discovers its irremediable shortcomings and places itself under the judgment of the Cross, it opens itself to genuine holiness. Everything "is implicitly related to the holy."[50] This relationship to holiness is revealed in man's discovery of the New Being. Then man's activity becomes holy. "Everything has the dimension of depth, and in the moment in which the third dimension is actualized, holiness appears."[51] There is no more sin, if by sin we understand "the unreconciled duality of ultimate and preliminary concerns . . . the state of things in which God is not 'all in all,' the state in which God is 'in addition to' other things."[52] There is no such duality now. God is all in all, because all one's actions, whatever their legalistic or moralistic medium, are directed to the Ultimate.

The ethics of the New Being develops a "sensitive" rather than "good" conscience. It implies liberation from moral commands as well as from moral prohibitions. Man's free inclination now determines his purposes. The liberty of the children of God creates a new morality in harmony with the New Being, and by so doing unveils the holiness of creation. And the holy is the sphere of the divine, in which the divine radiates. At this point, the mind that is accustomed to other concepts of ethical principles may well ask Tillich how this is possible: If the transmoral conscience follows no definite standard, how does it remain on the strait and narrow path that leads to the Kingdom of God?

48. *Ibid.*, p. 136.　　　　　49. *Systematic Theology* I, p. 217.
50. *Ibid.*, p. 218.　　　　　51. *Ibid.*
52. *Ibid.*

In a sermon on the transitoriness of life, Paul Tillich explains the concept of God's wrath. "God's anger is not directed against our moral shortcomings, against special acts of disobedience to the divine order. It is directed against the secret of our personality, against what happens in us and to us, unseen by men, unseen even by ourselves. This, our secret, determines our fate. . . ."[53] The transmoral conscience breaks this fatal cycle by changing our intimate secret. Of all the possible human attitudes, only one stands above judgment because it itself is judgment; only one is not condemned because everything is condemned and redeemed by it. This is love. The moralists of absolutism and the philosophers of relativism have both failed to find a lasting principle of ethics. Absolutism "breaks down in every radical change of history."[54] Relativism "makes change itself the ultimate principle."[55] Both are fallacious. Neither leads to the Kingdom of God. But there is a way between them. "Love, *agape*, offers a principle of ethics which maintains an eternal, unchangeable element but makes its realization dependent on continuous acts of creative intuition."[56]

No law is stable, for history shows that laws have changed. The only stable moral principle must be above the law. Such is love, "above the natural law in Stoicism and the supra-natural law in Catholicism."[57] Speaking in philosophical terms, Tillich justifies the lordship of love in a transmoral ethics: "*Love alone* can transform itself according to the concrete demands of every individual and social situation without losing its eternity and dignity and unconditional validity."[58] Love alone is able to determine standards of conduct that will respect the changing human situations while safeguarding the divine content of every human action in which man is ultimately concerned. *Systematic Theology* I contains a splendid page on the power of love to transform human actions. Love is an absolute law because it is also absolute self-sacrifice. As love it is absolute, eternally related to the ground of being and manifesting this ground in action. There is no danger of its swerving from the divine, because it is the

53. *The Shaking of the Foundations*, p. 72.   54. *The Protestant Era*, p. 154.
55. *Ibid.*   56. *Ibid.*, pp. 154-55.
57. *Ibid.*, p. 155.   58. *Ibid.*

divine. "Love is always love; that is its static and absolute side."[59]

Yet, love cannot degenerate into heteronomy and impose again the harsh burden of a law, for it is relative as well as absolute. "Love is always dependent on that which is loved, and therefore it is unable to force finite elements on finite existence in the name of an assumed absolute."[60] Combining the two elements, Tillich formulates the nature of love in striking phrases: "The absoluteness of love is its power to go into the concrete situation, to discover what is demanded by the predicament of the concrete to which it turns."[61] "It is absolute as love and relative in every love relationship."[62] The question should then be asked, Love of what? As seen by Tillich, love has two correlative poles: "the Unconditional and 'the other,' i.e. the other human being. . . . The Unconditional could be an illusion if it did not appear through the unconditional demand of the other *person* to acknowledge him as a person. And conversely, 'the other,' if he did not demand an *unconditional* acknowledgement of his personal dignity, could be used as a tool for my purposes."[63] The ethics of the New Being is essentially inter-personal. "Love is the drive toward the unity of the separated."[64]

In this, love is essentially Christological. The coincidence of relativity and absoluteness is the meaning of the Cross. The negation of self which goes out to the other to the full extent of love and thus reveals their underlying unity is the sacrifice of Jesus in which the Christ was manifested. In our relation to the Cross of the Christ we ecstatically perceive that "the paradox of the final revelation, overcoming the conflict between absolutism and relativism, is love."[65] Wherever love, rather than law and morality, dominates ethics, the Christ is manifested. The following sentence expresses the radically Christological character of the transmoral conscience: "The love of Jesus as the Christ, which is the manifestation of the divine love—and only this—embraces everything concrete in self and world."[66] In love, the absolute

59. *Systematic Theology* I, p. 152.   60. *Ibid.*
61. *Ibid.*   62. *Ibid.*, p. 153.
63. *Ibid.*, p. 216.   64. *Love, Power and Justice*, p. 25.
65. *Systematic Theology* I, p. 152.   66. *Ibid.*

becomes relational. Man is totally dominated by the divine ground of love, and totally committed to all other human beings.

When love reigns, the ethical problem is solved. The yoke of the law no longer exists. Moral pride has vanished. The "sin of religion" has come to an end.[67] No longer do men suffer "the arrogance of the Churches, the cruelty of the moralists and the inflexibility of the orthodox."[68] For the absoluteness of the moral obligation is counterbalanced by the relativity of love. Then "the right decision must sacrifice its claim to be the right decision. There are no right decisions; there are trials and defeats and successes. But there *are* decisions which are rooted in love, which by resigning the absolute do not fall into the relative. . . . No decision can be annihilated; no action can be undone. But love gives meaning even to those decisions and actions which prove to be failures. The failures of love do not lead to resignation but to new decisions beyond absolutism and relativism."[69] No objective law is absolute. What is absolute is this: life, as directed by the transmoral conscience, becomes the expression of un-conditional love. Love creates the forms in which it will express its divine ground. These forms may be successful or they may be failures; at any rate they are neither right nor wrong. They are beyond morality, in the realm of love's creativity.

The centre of the ethics of the New Being as described by Tillich is the supremacy of love over law. Love creates its forms, or it gives a divine content to forms of behaviour borrowed from human culture. The love in question is the love of God, God being understood in the sense of being-itself, not one being among others, but the Supreme Being. Such a love embraces all created beings as concrete expressions of being-itself. It is focused on the Christ as the manifestation of being-itself in the conditions of existence. There is a close kinship between this and the Catholic doctrine of the supremacy of love. Well known is the saying of St John of the Cross: "In the evening of your life, you shall be examined on love."[70] Conformity to the moral law will not

---

67. *The Shaking of the Foundations*, p. 49.   68. *Ibid.*
69. *Systematic Theology* I, pp. 152-53.   70. *Maxims*, n. 56.

decide eternal bliss or doom. Rather, the love of God that shall have informed both our obedience to the law and, if possible, our aberrations shall judge us. This is also a common doctrine of the Catholic mystics—that at the summit of spiritual life, the soul is entirely guided by the instinctive discoveries of its love of God. The higher one has been raised into the love of God, the more all-embracing is its light. What the mind learns through the commandments, love knows by experience. Then the law is transformed. No longer a yoke, it is a delight. Man no longer obeys an exterior, heteronomous authority; rather, he discovers anew the regulations of the law in the implications of his love.

Thomas Aquinas himself acknowledged the supremacy of love in Catholic ethics. In very strong formulas he expressed the principle that "every conscience, be it right or erroneous, is binding."[71] And conscience, in Thomistic ethics, is not only an intellectual knowledge of the laws. It is also the recipient of God's moral guidance through the gifts of the Holy Spirit. This guidance increases with growth in love. He who is totally committed to love always knows how to behave, even though he may be in the dark as to the letter of the law. "Frequently we do not know what to do or what to wish, but love teaches all that is necessary to salvation."[72] Love, if it is truly love, implies that in any problem or dilemma we shall be led by a spiritual instinct. For, "where love is, there is the Holy Spirit, who knows all, and who guides us in the strait path."[73]

These remarks are necessary to appreciate the ethics of Paul Tillich. Insofar as it is an ethics of love, it is sound. What it affirms is correct. Love is able to rise above the law; it does not follow, but leads, the law. The conscience of the mystics, enlightened by God's illuminations, may be called a transmoral conscience. It does not need to be told what the law is. For, consciously or not, it fulfils the law. In this respect Tillich's vehement denunciation of the burden and yoke of obedience meets the requirements of Catholic ethics, which must always be an ethics of purpose and intention, that is, of love.

71. *Quodl.* 3, a. 27.   72. *De Decem Praeceptis*, Ch. 3.
73. *Ibid.*

And yet there are negative elements in Tillich's system that fall short of the requirements of love. The contrast between love and law is largely artificial. For in the concrete situation of the Christian who is totally committed to God, love never contradicts the law: it fulfils it. Love invents the law if the law is not explicitly known, and what it invents always corresponds to the law, because both have the Holy Spirit as their inspirer. The moral law of nature or of revelation cannot contradict the true love of God; and the true love of God always desires to follow the moral law. In cases where the law is doubtful or difficult to know, love follows its own instinct, but always with the desire to be within the law. Catholic ethics affirms both the supremacy of love and the divine origin of an objective moral law. Tillich affirms the first and ignores the second. He separates what Catholicism unites.

There is a strange blindness in the position that Christological ethics must not preach the law. This assumes that Christians easily reach a point of total commitment where they may safely rely on the instinct of love—an amazing assumption for a theologian who believes that we are sinners in our very existence prior to any action or thought. Every teacher knows that correct behaviour does not come spontaneously. Even love has to be taught. One must learn to respect and understand others even when one really loves them. It is not easy to respect the secret of another person, even for one who is totally devoted to him. The Old Testament agreed with common sense when it stated that "the fear of God is the beginning of wisdom."[74] Christ did not abolish the law; he fulfilled it. Love likewise does not seek to be freed from laws, but to fulfil them. On this point we must disagree with Tillich's attitude. There is no true ethics of love that is not, first, an ethics of law. Admittedly, Tillich wishes to respect the relative value of the laws, and he only claims that the ethics of the New Being rises above them. Instead of falling into subjectivity, he believes that he goes beyond objectivity and subjectivity. However, this misrepresents the nature of love. Love soars above the law only to subject itself to the law again. Love is free, and it freely longs for

74. Psalm 90.10.

obedience. As soon as we speak of obedience, we must ask, Obedience to what? In the realm of ethics, obedience can only be to objective standards, that is, to laws. It would not do to say that in an interpersonal perspective, love obeys the unexpressed wishes of other persons without any law; for these wishes are obeyed by love only insofar as they are inscribed in the depth of being that personality implies, which amounts to saying that they are natural laws.

Catholic ethics, which upholds the supremacy of love, also maintains the objective absoluteness of divine and natural laws. In reproaching Catholicism for teaching an heteronomous morality, Tillich commits two fallacies. First, he overlooks the fact that Catholic ethics is centred on purpose, that is, on love. Second, he misunderstands the relations between love and law. Instead of rising, as he claims, above subjectivity and objectivity, he goes astray, after winding detours, into subjectivity. Yet, it is to Tillich's credit that he has seen the ideal of a truly religious ethics, and what he has perceived is precisely the Catholic vision. Tillich writes: "Love, realizing itself from *kairos* to *kairos*, creates an ethics which is beyond the alternative of absolute and relative ethics,"[75] a statement which unwittingly describes the ethical development of the Catholic Church. There, and only there, is no alternative, but a harmonious unity of the absolute and the relational. The tragedy of Paul Tillich and the inescapable doom of his theological construction is that he seeks for the transmoral conscience outside this unity. Again, it is the Catholic conception of morality that he describes in this encomium on theonomous ethics: "It avoids the destructiveness of the heteronomous way. . . . It asserts (in agreement with the predominant trend of classical theology) that the law given by God is man's essential nature, put against himself as law. . . . The law is not strange to man. It is natural law. It represents his true nature from which he is estranged. Every valid ethical commandment is an expression of man's essential relation to himself, to others and to the universe."[76] Tillich tries to build the theonomous ethics that he so adequately outlines, without noticing that it already exists, fully

75. *The Protestant Era*, p. 156.   76. *Love, Power and Justice*, pp. 76-77.

interpersonal and yet completely objective, in Catholic theology. His search is encumbered by confusing Catholicism and heteronomy. Trying to avoid heteronomy, he misses, in practice, the Catholic theonomy and falls into the fallacy of autonomous subjectivity.

Before leaving our topic we may subject this argument to a test. In *The Religious Situation* Tillich deplores the breakdown of sexual ethics in modern society. He rightly affirms that sex relations must necessarily be chaotic and spiritually frustrating unless an unconditional commitment underlies them. "Individuality can unite with individuality in living union only in the presence of a third, superior principle. And the only principle which is unconditionally super-ordinate is that which transcends time and change, the eternal. . . . This is one of the places where the misery of a self-sufficient finitude reveals itself in the tragic fate of countless individuals and where it demands that breaking-through to the transcendent on which sex morality can be built anew."[77] Tillich is not blind to the fact that Protestantism is partly responsible for this breakdown. Protestantism, he warns in *Systematic Theology* I, "is in danger . . . of cutting off the sexual realm from the ground of being and meaning in which it is rooted and from which it gets its consecration."[78]

Tillich also perceives the meaning of sex in the proper perspective. As a form of love it points to the fact that human beings are separated, estranged from each other, and it attempts to overcome estrangement through reunion. "It is the fulfilment and the triumph of love that it is able to reunite the most radically separated beings, namely individual persons."[79] The ethical question is, How can this reunion be achieved so that it takes place under the judgment of the eternal? It would seem to be consistent with Tillich's concern for Christian symbolism to mention the symbolic character of marriage, on account of which the Catholic tradition calls it a sacrament. Sexual union is ethical when it is

---

77. *The Religious Situation*, pp. 137-38.
78. *Systematic Theology* I, p. 119, n. 4.
79. *Love, Power and Justice*, p. 26.

truly a symbol of the reunion of what is estranged. No such reunion is adequately expressed except in indissoluble marriage. The supremacy of love is then respected. Love bows to the law of marriage because it itself demands such a law. We are in a theonomy, for the eternal dimension itself requires this form of union. Traditional standards of ethical morality are vindicated without any lapse, or relapse, into heteronomy and the yoke of the law.

This would be the Catholic way. Paul Tillich discards it. Indeed he strongly objects to "the principles which are supposed to control the sexual relations," for these are "historically conditioned and often in flagrant conflict with the intrinsic justice of these relations."[80] Thus, if we do not misread him, the principle of stable marriage and the principle that extra- or pre-marital relations do not fulfil "the intrinsic justice of these relations" are jeopardized. Instead of appealing to the eternal meaning of marriage, Tillich borrows his norm from psychological experience. "Love relations, most conspicuously relations between the sexes, remain without joy if we use the other one as a means for pleasure or as a means to escape pain. . . . Every human relation is joyless in which the other person is not sought because of what he is in himself, but because of the pleasure he can give us and the pain from which he can protect us."[81] This is perfectly true. Yet from this general remark no more can be inferred than that not all forms of sex relations give joy. It is a completely inadequate basis for developing a theonomous ethics of sex. True, Tillich invokes a standard, but this turns out to be purely subjective: "It is not an external law which warns us about certain forms of these relations, but the wisdom born out of past experiences which tells us that some of these relations may give pleasure, but that they do not give joy. They do not give joy because they do not fulfil what we are, and that for which we strive."[82] It would be logical to add, then, that no one can have such a wisdom unless he has ventured into sexual adventures for pleasure's sake and has been disappointed. Thus autonomy breeds disgust, but this is

80. *Ibid.*, p. 82.   81. *The New Being*, p. 146.
82. *Ibid.*

far from theonomy. I doubt that Tillich wants it so; yet he actually makes autonomy a necessary experience in the search for a theonomous ethics. In the sexual realm, still more than in others, this is catastrophic.

Tillich is unable to build a sexual ethics on his conception of the transmoral conscience. He perceives the principle. Seeking to apply it, he falls into pure subjectivity. Why this failure? Clearly, it has come about because Tillich conceives the transmoral conscience as escaping, rather than fulfilling, objective laws. That such laws exist and are derived from the impact of the ground of being upon all beings, he admits. That one should take them precisely as laws and pattern our behaviour on them, he denies for fear of heteronomy. On the contrary, the Catholicism of the great theologians avoids heteronomy without falling into autonomy; it fulfils both subjectivity and objectivity by uniting them in ethics.

It is true that the behaviour of Catholics is not always theonomous. Tillich is right when he notes that heteronomy plays a large part in Catholic ethics, but he mistakes its significance. Theonomous ethics belongs to the saints, to those whom the undeserved grace of God has raised to full spiritual freedom. Most of us are theonomous only at times, when we rise above our average. Our ethics, then, is a mixture: heteronomy, when we obey the law for no other reason than that it is the law; autonomy, when we escape the law and go on our own, experimenting with temptation and sin; theonomy, when we perceive that there is a higher realm, to which we obscurely aspire. In its belief-ful realism, the Catholic Church knows that, in this world, theonomy can only be achieved by way of obedience.

The praiseworthy element in Tillich's Christological ethics is that it eloquently shows the correlation of dogma and ethics. The specific character of his Christology, namely the definition of the Christ as essential Godmanhood appearing in existence, dominates his ethics too. To behave ethically, in this view, is to be ultimately concerned about the connection of our actions with essential Godmanhood. The dogmatic distortions of Tillich's Christology are faithfully copied in the corresponding ethics. The justification of the sinner, as now understood, determines the ethical orientation of theology. This is not an ethics of good works, or of the imitation of Christ, or of sacramental sanctification. It is an ethics of ontological participation. All being fundamentally partakes of being-itself. Being-itself is its fecund ground, the womb of all things. The symbolism of Christology points to being-itself. The historical aspects of Christology assume that being-itself has been manifested on earth in an ecstatic experience that escaped the distortions of estranged existence. The dogmas of Christology have been radically pared until nothing is left but the manifestation of being-itself in the Christ. The ethics of Christology have been similarly pruned of their legal and sacramental elements: all that remains is "faith," an ultimate concern, activity directed towards being-itself. This Christology, at least, is consistent.

Consistency, however, does not make such a synthesis sound. As we have seen, it is destructive of traditional dogmatics and of traditional ethics. Does it at least provide a solid basis for modern apologetics? This would seem to be Tillich's main concern. But apologetics is valid only if its purpose is to bring others to the faith once committed to the saints; it is fallacious if it radically reinterprets that faith away from its original meaning.

Is it still Protestantism? Tillich believes that his Christology alone safeguards the essence of Protestantism and, together with it, the essence of Christianity and of all religion. But the Reformers would hardly have recognized it. Tillich uses them occasionally as he uses the Fathers or Holy Writ, but always reinterpreting them in the light of his understanding of the Protestant principle. A Protestantism that has come to light only in the twentieth century can no more be Protestantism than a Christology discovered in the twentieth century can be the Christology of the Revelation.

Chapter VIII

TOWARDS A CHRISTOLOGY OF MAN

TO the question, "Whom do they say that I am?" Paul Tillich, after so many others, has given his answer. The Christ is eternal Godmanhood, the essence of man paradoxically appearing under the conditions of existence. All men have aspired to this revelation; they have longed for an escape from the dilemma of an existence which is never adequate to its essence. Their religions have attempted to find a way out of the human labyrinth. Among the Hebrews this expectation was more realistic than in other nations. They sought for no philosophical or academic solution. They envisaged the possibility, which became a hope and finally a certainty, that the dilemma could be solved by the appearance in time, within the weft of history, of a transcendent messenger in whom the divine and the human would be joined. The Messiah, the Christ, the Servant of Yahweh, the Prophet to come, the Son of Man, the Son of God, were some of the representations of this ideal messenger of salvation. The Christian faith consists in believing that this messenger has come: he took part in human history in a certain place, Galilee and Judea, at a certain time, "under Pontius Pilate," Governor of Judea, and his human name was Jesus of Nazareth. All men believe, more or less explicitly, in the Christ. For they all are aware of the existential problem and hope for a solution. Christians alone believe that the Christ, eternal Godmanhood, was in Jesus the man; that Jesus was the manifestation of the Christ.

This would be Tillich's formulation of the Christian faith. We have seen the implications of his Christology in the fields of symbolics, the interpretation of history, dogma and ethics. It remains to take a general view of Tillich's solution of the Christological problem.

Tillich has followed a way of his own in modern Protestant theology. His philosophical concerns are unique among theologians, and his constant tendency to reinterpret the older dogmas in ontological terms makes him a lone figure in the contemporary theological panorama. This has caused him to be harshly judged: "He seems neo-orthodox to the liberal theologian, liberal to the neo-orthodox, modernist to the fundamentalist, indiscriminately biblical to the modernist, historicist to the idealistic philosopher, and idealistic to the historicist."[1] Through his lectures and writings Tillich undoubtedly exerts a seminal influence on American Protestantism. His fame is at a peak. Even in the most unexpected quarters the urge to speak a Tillichian language is strong. Some of the warmest endorsements of his theology have even come from within the Episcopal Church. Yet one may surmise that the Fathers of the English Reformation would hardly have agreed with A. T. Mollegen's opinion that theological opposition to Tillich simply arises from a misunderstanding: "The biblical, Christocentric and critical character of Tillich's theology is not generally understood."[2] Also in the Episcopal Church, W. Norman Pittenger has fully endorsed the "Nestorian" elements of Tillich's Christology. His volume *The Word Incarnate* (1959) argues that the faith of Chalcedon is actually Nestorian and that a good Christology must follow the Patriarch of Constantinople deposed for heresy by the Council of Ephesus. This again is very close to one aspect of Tillich's thought.

Yet opposition is not a simple matter of misunderstanding. Between Tillich or his followers and orthodox Christology there is a substantial difference, of which the major Protestant theologians are aware. Their Christologies are far from the

---

1. A. T. Mollegen, "Christology and Biblical Criticism in Paul Tillich," in *The Theology of Paul Tillich*, p. 231. Other Anglican judgments are less favourable: J. V. Langmead Casserley, "Event-Symbols and Myth-Symbols" in *Crosscurrents*, vol. 8, n. 4, pp. 315-26; Wilfrid O. Cross, "Some Notes on the Ontology of Paul Tillich" in *Anglican Theological Review*, October, 1957, n. 4, pp. 297-310.
2. *Ibid.*, p. 231.

ontological interpretations in which Tillich finds a solution to all Christological problems.

Thus Rudolf Bultmann maintains the man Jesus, and not only the Apostles' interpretation of him as the Christ, at the centre of the Christian message. Demythologization itself is meant to define the relevance of Jesus for contemporary man, not to do away with him: Jesus and the core of his doctrine escape the category of myth.[3] At the other end of the theological spectrum, Karl Barth emphatically rejects any attempt to express the Christian faith in philosophical terms. Christology is not an answer to a previous question. The coming of Jesus the Christ is a totally gratuitous event, unanticipated by the human mind and irreducible to general categories.[4] The disagreements that occurred when several of Barth's early companions parted with him have been echoed in Tillich's thought. While Barth, in his *Church Dogmatics*, shows little concern with the theology of Paul Tillich, the latter has denounced the "supranaturalism" of Barth as a "self-deception"[5] and castigated what he calls—wrongly, it would seem—the "slumber of Barthianism with respect to the historical problem" of Jesus.[6]

Tillich seems closer to Emil Brunner, one of Karl Barth's former comrades-in-arms. With Brunner he emphasizes the relevance of the human question to which Christ provides the divine answer. Yet Brunner's fidelity to the Chalcedonian doctrine is a far cry from Tillich's indifference to it. Tillich could not have written: "Every attempt to destroy 'the' quality of His Being which is defined in the 'Two Natures' doctrine, weakens and finally completely destroys the scriptural belief in revelation."[7] This implies loyalty to what Tillich condemns as "supranaturalism," a rejoinder that Brunner could well call "a disastrous misunderstanding."[8]

3. Rudolf Bultmann, *Jesus and the Word*, 1934; *Theology of the New Testament*, 2 vols., 1952, 1955.
4. Karl Barth, *Kirchliche Dogmatik*, vol. 4, part 1 (1953); vol. 4, part 2 (1955); vol. 5, part 1 (1959).
5. *Systematic Theology* II, p. 12.
6. *Ibid.*, p. 102.
7. Emil Brunner, *The Mediator*, 1934, p. 248.

Tillich would find a better hearing among some Calvinist theologians who have little in common with Calvin's staunch orthodoxy in Christological matters. To the late John Baillie in his early period, the reasoning of Leo's tome to Flavian, which was approved by the Council of Chalcedon, seemed "entirely perverse."[9] Baillie was too optimistic in his assessment of modern theology: the doctrine of the two natures, he believed, "has been definitely abandoned by what is certainly a majority of those who in our day have devoted independent reflection to this whole matter."[10] John Baillie's brother, Donald, walked on hardly more traditional ground with his *God Was in Christ* (1947). The "perennial task of theology," as he understood it, is "to think out the meaning of the Christian conviction that God was incarnate in Jesus, that Jesus is God and man."[11] Donald Baillie found no fault with the doctrine of the two natures of Christ, though he rejected the correlative doctrine of the one Person.[12] His objections to the latter betrayed the same "Nestorian" traits that have been observed in Tillich. For Donald Baillie, the problem of the human and the divine in Christ was analogous to a similar problem in us. Our goodness is not ours, it is God's. Christ is perfect goodness, and so he is perfectly God. We are good because God lives in us by grace; and Jesus was perfect goodness because God was perfectly in him, so perfectly that Jesus was God. This argument comes very close to Tillich's Christology. Whereas Tillich pursues it at the ontological level of being, Baillie followed it at the moral level of the good.

Turning now to the greatest biblical Christology of our time, that of Oscar Cullmann, we find practically no common ground with Paul Tillich. In *Christ and Time* (1950) and in *The Christology of the New Testament* (1960), Cullmann analyses the thought-cate-

---

8. Brunner applies this to "the modern interpretation of the dogma of the divine nature of Christ" as put forward by Ritschl and Harnack. This criticism is equally valid as regards Tillich's interpretation. See *The Mediator*, pp. 249–64.

9. John Baillie, *The Place of Jesus Christ in Modern Christianity*, 1929, p. 127.

10. *Ibid.*, p. 130.

11. Donald Baillie, *God Was in Christ*, p. 83.

12. *Ibid.*, pp. 85–93.

gories of the primitive Church concerning Christ. There is no question of separating, as Tillich insists on doing, Jesus the historical man from the interpretation of him by the early Christians. The essence of Christological heresy lies precisely in effecting such a separation: "Docetism (i.e., the Christological solution in which Jesus' historical work as such is not the centre of God's whole revelation) is branded already in the New Testament as the fundamental Christological heresy. Anyone who does not confess that Jesus Christ has come in the flesh belongs to the Antichrist. As soon as the centre of revelation is no longer the Christ who appeared in the flesh, we cease to move on the level of New Testament Christology."[13] These lines were presumably written without any conscious reference to Paul Tillich. They are all the more impressive. Tillich's Christology can spare the historical Jesus. It is not so much focused on a historical event as on a philosophico-religious principle.

There would therefore seem to be a growing consensus of most contemporary Protestant theologians who work in the field of Christology, that Tillich's approach is deficient, not to say misleading. It is not biblical enough, not historical enough, not theological enough. It develops a philosophy of a Hegelian type,[14] rather than a theology. Its praiseworthy attempt to "correlate" the human quest for the Christ and the answer given by God in the Christ has failed. For the answer is so determined by the question that the gratuitous character of the Christ disappears together with his uniqueness. We have a diluted Christology which might be acceptable to a Hindu or a Buddhist: they can accept everything in Tillich's exposition, except precisely the fact that Jesus himself and no other was, and is, and ever shall be, the Christ. But the latter point is not essential to the notion of eternal Godmanhood appearing in existence. Tillich the believer believes it as a fact, while Tillich the systematic theologian relegates it to a secondary place.

Sharp as these criticisms may be, they cannot eliminate the

13. Oscar Cullmann, *The Christology of the New Testament*, p. 324.
14. See Mollegen; *loc. cit.*, p. 231, quoting Emil Brunner.

central problem raised by Tillich's ontological Christology. It is not enough to say, with one of his most outspoken critics, that "such a system as this cannot long endure if confronted with the marvellous revelation given in the Word of God."[15] We should try to salvage what we can of Tillich's valuable insights in order to incorporate them in an orthodox Christology. The central problem he raises is likely to remain with us for a long time: Is it possible to express the Christian faith in other than the categories of nature and person which the Council of Chalcedon canonized? Whatever strictures we could formulate concerning his system, this question is valid. It has been raised before. No one, however, has done it with the earnestness and insistence of Tillich. If we want to be understood when we speak of the Christ, we should use another problematic than that of the fifth century. The question of this new problematic may not be soluble, yet it is legitimate to formulate it.

Saying this does not amount to accepting Paul Tillich's criticism of, and his departure from, the Council of Chalcedon. To a Catholic, and to the Protestant who feels bound by tradition, the Council of Chalcedon remains the greatest attempt to express the dogma of the Incarnation in intelligible terms that respect the ultimate mystery of the coming of God in the flesh. It constitutes a norm for our theology. He who abandons this norm will go astray.

Yet this does not imply that the vocabulary and the problematic of Chalcedon are the best possible. It was imperative for the Church Fathers to solve the Christological dilemma in terms of nature and person, because the dilemma had itself been formulated in relation to those terms. But Tillich rightly remarks that modern philosophy and theology have little concern for the Greek interest in *ousia, prosopon, hupostasis*. Oscar Cullmann himself, who does not see eye to eye with Paul Tillich on any major Christological question, believes that "the problem of the two natures of Christ" is "logically insoluble."[16]

Tillich's desire to express Christology in terms of history

15. R. Allan Killen, *The Ontological Theology of Paul Tillich*, 1946, p. 139.
16. *Ibid.*, p. 192.

rather than in terms of nature remains unsatisfactory, for it does not take the dogma of Chalcedon seriously enough to earn the right of criticism. Tillich will have no "higher chemistry between finiteness and infinity."[17] To his mind, this is what the doctrine of Chalcedon amounts to. Yet the Church Fathers deserve better than this. We should pay them the compliment of considering them too intelligent to have tried to express a divine mystery "in terms of a higher chemistry."

Tillich's own position falls short of a solution. The question, validly formulated, is couched in historical terms: What is the relation between an event of history, the appearance of the Christ, and universal salvation? The Christian answer was given in a historical event. How are the two related?

Tillich's answer, however, is not historical, but ontological. The New Being underlies all being. It has the power to relate all being to its eternal Ground and Abyss. Its appearance in existence establishes such a relation. It is the manifestation of essence-in-existence, the transcending of estrangement from self and from the eternal Ground of all. Wherever the New Being appears, salvation is achieved. The coming of the Christ is such a break-through of the New Being. Others can be thought of or hoped for. This particular manifestation of the New Being is the norm of Christianity because it is the greatest manifestation that has ever been perceived.

Such a solution is no solution. For the historical problem remains untouched: Why and how is Jesus the Christ? Why and how is this particular limited man the channel of eternal and universal Godmanhood? Tillich's ontological answer explains a possibility. It does not justify the concrete fact that Jesus and none other is the Christ, eternal Godmanhood, essence under the conditions of existence and yet conquering existence. The passage from ontology to history has not been made. Can it be made?

A first requirement for passing from an ontological to a historical Christology would be to discover whether the philo-

---

17. "A Reinterpretation of the Doctrine of the Incarnation" in *Church Quarterly Review* (London, England), No. 294, Jan.-March 1949, p. 139.

sophical notion of eternal Godmanhood corresponds to any of the prophetic categories of the expectation of a Saviour as found in the Old Testament. Among the many forms that this expectation took, the "Son of Man" of Daniel 7.13 ff. seems to fit well enough. It is nowadays admitted that "Son of Man" is too literal a translation of the Aramaic *bar nascha*, which would be better rendered by the single word "man." The *bar nascha* who appears to Daniel on the clouds is simply *the Man*. The expression is to be understood collectively. Though later Judaism, as in the fourth Book of Esdras and in the Book of Enoch, understood it as an individual, concrete man, he represents and antedates mankind.[18] *The Man* has a pre-existence.

Oscar Cullmann convincingly shows that, of all the messianic titles, Jesus claimed the title of *the Man* more definitely than any other.[19] In 1 Corinthians 15.45-7, in Romans 5.12 ff. and in Philippians 2.5-11, St Paul developed the idea of *the Man* and identified "the heavenly Man," "the second Adam," "the second Man," with the concrete man Jesus. *The Man* is "from heaven."[20] He is spiritual, as contrasted with the first Adam, who was earthy. He appeared on earth as Jesus of Nazareth.

These, and other texts of the New Testament, impose the following conclusion: The early Church initiated a Christology in which Jesus was considered to be the incarnation of a pre-existing celestial Man. In spite of its scriptural basis (or perhaps largely because of its biblical categories), this Christology gradually disappeared in Greek territory. Yet Cullmann believes that the Christology of St Irenaeus of Lyons is a direct offshoot: "His entire Christology is dominated by the contrast between Adam and Christ, and he makes the only attempt in the whole history of doctrine to build a Christology on the concept 'Man.' "[21]

18. On all this, see Cullmann, *loc. cit.*, pp. 137-52.   19. *Ibid.*, pp. 152-64.
20. 1 Cor. 15.47. On St Paul, see Cullmann, *loc. cit.*, pp. 167-81. Lucien Cerfaux, in *Christ in the Theology of St Paul* (1959), is extremely reserved concerning the expression, Son of Man; this seems to be due to an apologetic attitude fearing the possible connections between a theology of the Son of Man and the cosmogonic myth of the primordial Man.
21. Cullmann, *loc. cit.*, p. 189.

The Man, the "celestial Man," is equal with God.[22] A post-Nicaean Christology that would take this as a scriptural basis would have to describe the Three Persons as the Father, the Man, the Spirit. In examining the meaning of "the Man," it might follow the patristic line of thought according to which man's essence is to be the image, the *eikon*, of God. The second Person, the Man-God, is the perfect Image of the Father, of whom he is eternally born. It is precisely that which makes him the pre-existent Man. To be a man on earth consists in being destined to imitate this Man, in being created an image of God. All men are types of this eternal Archetype, of the Image of the Father, of *the Man*. Mankind is thought out in God neither as a collection of individual creatures, nor even as creaturely in the first place. *The Man* is God himself, the Son. Mankind is *man*kind only by participation in the divine Likeness, in the divine Man.

A post-Chalcedonian Christology can be developed along these lines. What the Council of Chalcedon, using a Greek vocabulary, called the two natures, divine and human, of Christ, we should call the two humanities of Jesus: the divine Humanity, which is God himself, the eternal Exemplar of all images of God; and the creaturely humanity, in whose shape the divine Humanity appeared on earth at a given moment of history. These two are one—one "person" in the Chalcedonian language—by way of exemplarity: the creaturely humanity of Jesus is the perfect created likeness of the divine Man. In order to avoid Nestorian implications, we should not speak of Jesus as two men, but as two humanities—divine and human—in one man, the pre-existent divine Man. In order to avoid Monophysite misunderstandings, we should insist on the integrity of the creaturely humanity assumed by the eternal Man, "in all things like his brethren."[23] The philosophical difficulty of explaining the coexistence of two natures in Christ, and the psychological problem raised by the coexistence of a human psyche with a divine knowledge might both be bypassed: the Exemplar itself is, eternally so, divine and yet human, the divine Man. This could conceivably open the

22. Phil. 2.6.
23. Hebr. 2.17.

door to a solution of the ever-recurrent problem of the knowledge of Christ.[24]

Such a Christology would be scriptural. It would be seriously grounded in the patristic tradition. By respecting the relation of the divine and the human in Christ, which the Council of Chalcedon defined, it would be in keeping with Catholic orthodoxy.

I have briefly sketched a Christology of *the Man*. A full elaboration would require a separate volume. Yet it would seem that such a Christology can be constructed within the framework of traditional orthodoxy. We ought now to return to Tillich: can a Christology of the eternal Man be used to correct Tillich's Christology? Or, conversely, can Tillich's Christology be used to build up a Christology of *the Man*?

The main deficiency in the Tillichian solution is, as we have seen, that it provides no definite passage from the philosophical conception of "eternal Godmanhood" to the concrete existence of the man Jesus. "Jesus who is understood to be the Christ" is a conveniently hazy expression veiling a basic dilemma: How can the historical also be the eternal? How can Jesus, the man of Nazareth, be the Christ, the Ground of Being?

Paul Tillich's mistake lies in the concept of "eternal Godmanhood." Conceived as a universal, it can never fully and exclusively be identified with any particular event: the Christ (a universal) cannot be directly apprehended as Jesus (a concrete man): the eternal cannot be the historical. It appears in history only as the interpretation of a certain *kairos*. Paradoxically yet conceivably it may undergo the conditions of existence. This constitutes its revelation; but the conclusion that a concrete human being is indeed essence appearing in existence is reached in a subsequent ecstasy: the

24. "It would have the advantage of putting the logically insoluble problem of the two natures of Christ on a level where a solution becomes visible: the pre-existent Son of Man, who is with God already at the very beginning and exists with him as his image, is *by his very nature* divine Man. From this point of view the whole toilsome discussion which dominated the earlier Christological controversies actually becomes superfluous" (Cullmann, *loc. cit.*, p. 192).

ecstatic perception of the Apostles revealed the Christ in Jesus. What Jesus knew about it is irrelevant. Thus the eternal always escapes history. Jesus is known to have been the Christ after he has vanished. The Christ survives in the faith of the Apostles. Jesus is no longer important.

This dichotomy between the historical and the eternal is unbridgeable by Tillich's method. Yet there would be no dichotomy, if the divine element in the Christ were presented, not as a universal principle ("eternal Godmanhood"), but as a concrete Being who is, by essence, human in his very divinity. There is no "eternal Godmanhood," except in an eternal Godman. The eternal Godman, the Word, the Son of God, appears as a historical man. At this point, the dialectic of eternity and history would have a different function than in Tillich's system. There is now no problem of passing from the universal to the concrete, for the passage is from the eternally concrete to the historically concrete. This leaves us with no ultimate dilemma, because the passage is not effected at the historical moment of the Incarnation when the Word became flesh. It is effected in the very essence of *the celestial Man*: the Exemplar of historical man can enter the history of man, since the history of man is only a participation in his divine Humanity.

Admittedly, some of these ideas would need to be carefully defined. But this is not the place to build an entire Christology. All I have wished to do in this concluding chapter is to show that, after due correction, the Christology of Paul Tillich can be integrated in an orthodox Christology. A radical re-interpretation of the central conception of "eternal Godmanhood" is made possible by the Scriptures themselves and by the early tradition of the Church. It may be achieved in complete fidelity to the normative Councils of the early Church.

If this were done, then Tillich's effort to reinterpet the Christ to our contemporaries would not be in vain. His desire to correlate the question raised by man's existence and the answer given in the manifestation of the eternal would be fulfilled. For a Christology of *the celestial Man* would constitute a vantage ground for an integration of modern science and theology. Recent developments in paleontology, anthropology, sociology, depth-psychology, and phenomenology have provided us with new insights into the nature of man and with a language that was unknown to the older anthropology. The lasting elements of these sciences should take their place in a theological anthropology representing above all a study of the man Jesus as *the divine Man* appearing in the midst of creaturely mankind, a brother among brothers.

Jesus the Christ is the Saviour. In the language of medieval theologians, this implies that all sciences may be "reduced" to him; all contribute to the elaboration of Christology. Jesus the Christ is the mediator in all things. Though the Christology of Paul Tillich cannot express this insight with fidelity to the Church's tradition, nevertheless it does call for a reflection on Jesus the Christ that will be utterly committed to the full Christian tradition, and totally steeped in the anguish and the hope of our times.

The "new image of man" is itself an image—distorted no doubt, yet only partially so—of the eternal Man, the Son of God, to whom alone belong the Kingdom, the Power and the Glory.

INDEX

Jesus the Christ has been omitted as the whole book is devoted to Tillich's doctrine of the New Being in Jesus as the Christ.

175